Praise for The Knackere

'Love love love this book. It doesn't just simplify wine, it simplifies life. Essential reading.'   India Knight

'Raise a glass to this deliciously simple guide.' *Daily Mail*

'Presented in a humorous, chatty style this book is an intelligent, hugely informative wine guide and McGinn is certainly well qualified to pass on advice.'   *Daily Express*

'Useful, interesting and very funny – every woman who owns a corkscrew or knows about screw-caps needs a copy of this book.'

Victoria Moore, author of *The Wine Dine Dictionary*

'Call it a wine book if you will. It's also a book about contemporary parenthood. I heartily recommend it.'

Jewish Chronicle

'Her accessible and entertaining guide takes us through a 'school year' of simple wine lessons from an autumn term of cosy fireside reds to a summer 'love-in' of fruity outdoor favourites.'   *Lancashire Evening Post*

Helen McGinn is the author of award-winning wine blog The Knackered Mother's Wine Club. She has a weekly wine column in the *Daily Mail* and regularly appears on television as a wine expert. She's won numerous awards for her blog, including Fortnum & Mason's Online Drink Writer of the Year and *Red* magazine's Best Blogger. Helen spent almost a decade sourcing wines from around the world as a supermarket wine buyer before spending the next half-decade pregnant. She is married with three children, too many dogs and a weird cat. Her desert island wine would be a bottle of 1988 vintage champagne. Her desert island dish would not be left-over fish fingers.

Website: knackeredmotherswineclub.com
Instagram @knackeredmother
Facebook/knackeredmotherswineclub
Twitter @knackeredmutha

HELEN McGINN

THE KNACKERED Mother's WINE GUIDE

Because life's too short to drink bad wine

bluebird
books for life

First published 2013 by Macmillan

First published in paperback 2014 by Pan Books
This edition first published 2020 by Bluebird
an imprint of Pan Macmillan
The Smithson, 6 Briset Street, London EC1M 5NR
Associated companies throughout the world
www.panmacmillan.com

ISBN 978-1-5290-3020-4

Previously published as *The Knackered Mother's Wine Club*

1 3 5 7 9 8 6 4 2

A CIP catalogue record for this book is available from the British Library.

Designed and set by seagulls.net
Printed and bound by CPI Group (UK) Ltd, Croydon, CR0 4YY

Visit **www.panmacmillan.com** to read more about all our books
and to buy them. You will also find features, author interviews and
news of any author events, and you can sign up for e-newsletters
so that you're always first to hear about our new releases.

FOR TIM

CONTENTS

A chap called Hawker wrote a book called *Chats About Wine* back in 1907 and asked:

'. . . what is it? This wonderful elixir of life, which is almost as old as the world itself and yet is overflowing with the exuberance of youth; which restores and invigorates us when the powers of life are low; uplifts and cheers us in days of sorrow and gloom; evokes and enhances our joys and pleasures; and by which the inherent living force it is endowed with, gives animation, energy and inspiration to every sense and faculty we possess?'

That's wine, that is. And it is (mostly) delicious. You've just got to choose wisely.

INTRODUCTION

The **Knackered Mother** (*knackeredus maternius*) is most commonly seen in her natural habitat: the kitchen. Here, she slaves away putting food on the table for her children to flick all over the floor, occasionally falling silent to eat some of it herself. She exists on a diet of sandwich crusts, leftover fish fingers and KitKats with the odd half-cup of lukewarm tea if she's lucky. In daylight hours, when not with her cubs, she can be found manically trying to squeeze a week's work into three days whilst trying not to let the noise of small children, a needy dog and a weird cat be heard through the study door. At night, she can be found lying on the sofa, glass of (usually very good) wine within reach, trying to summon up the energy to cook/speak.

Not to be confused with the lesser-spotted **Shattered Father** (*bearded grumpius paternius*). There have been reported sightings of these creatures in the same habitat, but in each instance at least one of them was asleep.

* * *

I'm going to assume you are reading this because you are, like me, a knackered mother and/or a wine lover. This book is designed to help you explore, discover and, ultimately, choose wine with confidence. It's about ensuring that when you do decide to settle down with a glass of wine after a busy day, having wrestled the kids into bed, it's going to be worth it. The Knackered Mother's Wine Club just sort of, well . . . happened (I'll explain in a minute). It's not a very exclusive club to say the least, but basically, if you like wine, you're in: no dress code, no membership policy, no fees (other than buying this, obviously).

On the shelf in my study at home is a row of long-emptied wine bottles, each one marked with a date and occasion in silver pen, including a bottle of 1988 Vintage Champagne that marks the year the Husband and I got together as teenagers. It was a wedding present and we drank it years later, to celebrate the birth of Eldest Boy. I haven't been lucky enough to have it since, but I'll never forget how I felt when I drank it (clue: not knackered). The thing is, I love wine. Really love it. And I don't just mean what's in the glass. Obviously that's a really big part, and I love that there's always more to discover, but for me wine is about so much more than that. It's about bringing us together around a table, covered with food (or at the very least a bowl of crisps). Wine makes us sit down (I especially like that part) and converse. Wine connects us with places, with stories and, best of all, with each other.

Almost twenty years ago I decided I'd like to make my working way in the world with glass in hand, literally, because I liked what was in the glass. Now, a few years on, I can see that it wasn't just about that, it was as much about the people; those who make wine and those who drink it.

One of my favourite nights in my not particularly social calendar these days is my book-club evening. Sure, we talk about the book, but really it's about a group of friends getting together around a table, sharing funny, sad, mad and sometimes very bad stories, mixed in with opinions, food and – of course – a really nice glass of wine.

I've spent my entire working life in the wine industry, feeling for much of it that, like Charlie Bucket, I'd won the golden ticket. For years I was a supermarket wine buyer, and when the first of my three children came along I gave up the travel for the travel cot, and now work part-time in wine. Friends have always asked me for wine recommendations, whether it's for everyday drinking, slightly posh dinners, parties, weddings, christenings/naming days, anniversaries or big birthdays ending in a zero. And they've always told me how the great wall of wine they face each week in the supermarket can feel utterly overwhelming.

Consequently, for years I sent a regular email to friends who'd asked for recommendations, especially on good wine deals, and the title of that email was 'The Knackered Mother's Wine Club'. And that was where it all started; the blog was born one night when the Husband was away and I'd had enough of working late with the laptop on the sofa in front of the telly. I thought that sharing my own weekly wine purchases – two wines a week, whatever I happened to be drinking – might help inspire others to try something different as well as unearth some hidden gems and properly good deals along the way.

I blogged every week – usually with a glass in reach – whatever my mood: happy, not so happy or just plain knackered. For the first few months the blog was read religiously; by my sister, mother and the Husband. Then I started to get comments from people who were a) not related to me and b) interested in wine and wanting to know more about it. And so the weekly posts continued, with added videos and tasting tips, amongst other stuff. I received emails from women telling me they'd never realized Chablis was made from Chardonnay grapes (fact) or that 'legs' on a glass was a sign of alcohol content rather than quality. In short, my blog had hit on something.

These were busy, knowledge-thirsty (mostly) mothers, reading my blog and enjoying learning more about wine. It was a revelation. My audience started to grow, and suddenly there I was, doing what I love, namely sharing my thoughts on good wine and helping others grow in confidence when choosing, buying and talking about wine, whilst encouraging them to try new things.

How I drink now is very different to how I drank before I had children, not least because looking after children with a hangover is rarely worth the pain. More than that, as I get older I'm realizing that, actually, I don't want to drink as much as I used to. The shallow part of me knows the extra calories go straight to my jowls, the less shallow part of me knows that it isn't good for my general health. The rise in the number of drinkers doing dry spells, whether it's Dry January or Sober October, shows I'm not alone. Personally I'm more 'little and often' than 'all or nothing' but however you choose to approach it, mindful drinking is here to stay.

The recommended* weekly allowance is fourteen units. For me, that's about seven to ten glasses of wine a week, depending on the strength of the wine and the size of the glass. Pre-children, that was my weekend right there (sound familiar?). Nowadays, I go wine-free at least two nights a week. Overall, I drink less but I drink better. By that, I mean that instead of drinking the same wine week in, week out, I shop around and try different things whenever possible. With so much choice on the shelves and online, you could try a different wine every week and still only taste the tip of the wine-iceberg.

It is my hope that the information in this book will help you step outside your wine comfort zone and give you the knowledge you need to get more from your glass of wine, to take you beyond the discount deals and lead you by the hand – or perhaps the nose – through what to drink with

---

* NHS

Sunday roasts, children's parties (yes, children's parties and just for the grown ups, obviously), to book-club tastings, TV dinners, store-cupboard essentials and more. You will feel inspired not to drink more wine, that I should be clear on, but to drink *better* wine. I'm going to help you think about tasting wines properly, learn how to make tasting notes and not feel like a pretentious wine-freak writing down what you do and don't like. We're going beyond the bland to a newly discovered blend. I've written this with a very clear intention: to help you make more informed choices when selecting a bottle to drink, because, as we've already established, life's too short to drink bad wine.

Think of this as the start of term at your new wine school. With your pencil case, sharpened pencil and new book in front of you, we'll start with the essentials, namely what you need to have in your fridge door/on the side in the kitchen when the kids are all – finally – in bed. Then we'll look at some basics, including how wine is made. We'll move through the autumn term with fireside reds and store-cupboard essentials, before hitting the Christmas holidays with all you need to know to emerge wine-victorious over the festive period. Then we'll have a dry January and look at some alternatives to elderflower bloody cordial (unless it's Mrs Mills' – more on that later) before talking book-club wines and possibly sperm washing (don't ask). After that, we'll have a half-term break before learning all about what wines to drink with what roasts (it is coming up to Easter, after all). Then we'll do grown-up parties, having covered children's parties earlier, before getting ready for summer. Here, we'll cover school fêtes, barbecues in the garden and how to avoid bad holiday wine. By the time we break up for summer, you'll be all set with wine knowledge to dazzle your friends/husband/partner/parents/in-laws and, best of all, delight you. Ready?

CHAPTER
ONE

FRIDGE-DOOR WHITES AND IN-THE-RACK REDS

Wine is an excellent thing. After a typical day – school runs, a supermarket trolley-dash and possibly a conference call in which I try not to let on that I have a 3-foot-tall Power Ranger standing before me – I don't have the mental capacity for much beyond a glass of wine and easy conversation. Something delicious to kick the taste buds does more for me than Berocca ever could.

But before we go any further, I must address the issue of frazzled mums collapsing on the sofa, glass in hand. Hands up, that's me. But I am a normal person who likes a glass of wine. I'm not guzzling the bottle. They say women should know their limits. Well, I know mine. It's fourteen units a week. Sometimes I drink less than that, sometimes a bit more, but generally wine is part of everyday (or rather night) life in this house, usually served with food and chat, depending on how worn out we are, or with an episode of *Masterchef/Bake-Off* (delete as appropriate).

Mothers of old drank gin when pregnant and blew smoke in the other direction when holding a baby. We've come a long way since then and shouldn't be made to feel guilty just because we love a glass of wine at the end of the day. Motherhood already comes with a side order of guilt, and so, on behalf of all of us who drink responsibly, I'm sending that particular side order back. This book is about helping you to understand more about wine so that, seeing as you are probably drinking *less* than you used to, you make each glass count and drink *better*.

Now, any given day with small children generally involves tears, laughter and endless trips to the loo. And that's just me. The point is, motherhood is a joy but it is also completely exhausting. Along with the sheer pleasure and wonder our children bring us on a daily basis (don't they?), we are also faced with the slightly less joyful tasks of endless piles of washing to sort out, running a canteen and taxi service, wiping noses and bottoms and kitchen tables whilst picking up random bits of plastic as we go. Motherhood ain't no place for sissies, as they say. It is chaotic, messy and very, very noisy. But when the day is done, and the children are put to bed with clean faces and full tummies, I love the quiet that descends. Like a blanket, it gently tucks itself over the house. (I'd love to say this happens by 7.30p.m. every night, but what with the endless faffing of last-minute loo trips and missing teddies it's usually later than that.) Anyway, when it does finally happen, the quiet is restorative. It's grown-up time, and a glass of wine marks the split between the rest of our day and the time we have to ourselves in the evening.

I don't have a glass of wine every evening, but more often than not I do. And if I'm going to have a glass of wine I want it to be one worth drinking, not something that is instantly forgettable. Buying the same on-offer Pinot Grigio week in, week out, might give us the bargain-hit we crave, but it doesn't give us a thrill on the tongue. I'd rather open a better-than-average bottle during the week and make it last longer than have a cheap wine I 'don't mind' drinking.

HOW MUCH DO YOU NEED TO SPEND?

The wines in my fridge door and in the rack change every week. In the old days, when I worked for a big supermarket as a wine buyer, I had to taste at least forty wines a day to make sure everything was as it should do. I know, tough, huh? Brilliantly, this meant that I rarely had to buy wine with my own money; I just took it home from the office (with permission – I didn't steal it, I hasten to add).

Not having that luxury now, I have become an expert at shopping around, finding good deals and avoiding bad ones (sadly, some really are too good to be true – more on that later). Now that it's our own hard-earned cash I'm parting with, I'm generally far fussier. It had better be good. Having said that, we're feeding and clothing more people than we used to in this house, so money is very much an object.

If you spend £5 on a bottle of wine, *more than half of that cost* accounts for the duty and tax, leaving you with not much to spend on the actual wine, not even 50p in fact (after shipping and the retail mark-up). When you think how much you might spend nowadays on a cup of coffee or some emergency chocolate, 50p seems cheap by comparison. It follows that as the cost of the bottle rises, so does the quality of the wine. This is not always the case, but generally it's true. Once you get to £7 you are getting more than double the value in actual wine compared with that £5 bottle (I *know!*). Spend £10 and it doubles again. Spend £20 and half the cost accounts for the actual wine. Beyond £20 and you are buying something that is probably in limited supply and is priced by desire. Obviously, only you know how much you are willing to spend and if that wine is worth it to you. I generally shop for wine costing between £6 and £15, depending on what the wine is for and what my budget is.

When it comes to selecting our fridge-door whites and in-the-rack reds, these are wines we're likely to drink at home during the week, rather than wines we might bring out when eating with friends or family at the weekend (which we'll come to later). I really want to inspire you to try new wines and break out of your comfort zone. This is about how to have wines on hand that are a delight to drink, not just something that is drunk and forgotten.

Given that all wine starts the same way, as a grape on the vine, we need to explore what makes wines taste so very different. That way you can start to navigate your way around, allowing you to find the good stuff and avoid the bad. So don your metaphorical lab coat and geek specs; it's time to look at what's inside the bottle.

WHAT'S IN A WINE?

Grapes: whoever thought so much joy could come from such a small but perfectly formed fruit? Each grape just hangs out on the vine until ripe, ready to be picked and popped into our mouths – unless they are picked to make wine, which is obviously much more fun. Grapes are made up largely of **water**. It's all the other stuff in there that makes the grape great for wine. There are **natural sugars;** there are **flavours** that vary depending on the variety; and there is **natural acidity**. Another ingredient delivered with that little package is **tannin**.

WHAT IS TANNIN?

Tannin is one of the ingredients – a polyphenolic compound, to give it its proper definition – that makes up a grape. They are found on the skins, stalks and seeds of a grape, and how tannins are managed during the winemaking process has a very big influence on the resulting wine. If you are wondering what I mean by tannin, think of the feeling you get in your mouth when you take a sip of that cup of tea you made, the one where you got distracted by something or someone (probably small), and by the time you got back to your tea the teabag/tea leaves had been in for a bit too long, leaving it stewed and lukewarm. The relevant thing to remember is the bitter, astringent character of that fated cuppa. I realize I'm not selling tannin well here, but in wine it plays a crucial role as it preserves the wine, enabling it to age well.

When making red wine, the skins of the grapes are left in contact with the clear (almost always clear, no matter what the colour of the grape is) juice so that colour (aka anthocyanins) and tannins can be extracted. Generally, the thicker the skin of the grape, the more colour and tannin it will give to the grape juice.

Tannins come in different guises: 'big' tannins are often found in wines that are big in every other way, especially fruit and alcohol, such as New World Cabernet Sauvignon and Shiraz, and Malbec from Argentina. 'Firm' is a word often used to describe a wine where the tannins are very obvious, perhaps even a little harsh, as is sometimes found in very young wines. 'Soft' tannins are found in wines made from grapes with thinner skins, such as Gamay, Merlot or Pinot Noir, so the resulting tannins are lighter than their thick-skinned friends.

The best way to understand the difference tannins make to a wine is to try a 'big' tannin wine next to a 'soft' tannin wine; take a French Pinot Noir and taste it next to an Australian Shiraz. Be sure to taste the Pinot Noir first, then the Shiraz. Note how different the wine feels in weight. Obviously there are loads of other differences to take into account, such as the fruit characters, how much alcohol they have or whether they have been aged in oak barrels (since these also add tannin to a wine) but the 'feel' of the tannins will be incredibly different.

The essential ingredient is, of course, **alcohol**. Alcohol isn't in a grape when picked, but when nature's party trick happens, otherwise known as fermentation, yeasts convert the natural sugars in the grape to alcohol. That's some party trick. Mine's fitting my fist in my mouth; not that impressive by comparison, granted.

Oak, or rather the flavour of oak, is another ingredient that might be found in a wine. If a wine is aged in oak barrels, flavours and tannins from the oak will shape the wine over time. Oak is often wine's walking stick, allowing it to age gracefully and keeping it standing much longer than it otherwise would. So there we go. Water, sugar, flavours, acidity, tannin, alcohol and sometimes oak are what's in a wine. We'll explore all of these things in more detail as we go, but for now, that's a good place to start.

WHERE IN THE WORLD?

Billions of bottles of wine are made around the world every year and they are often categorized as being either from the Old World (meaning, generally speaking, wines from European countries) or from the New World (meaning wines from everywhere else, including Australia, New Zealand, Chile, Argentina and South Africa). Someone once described the difference in terms of style: Old World for more subtle wines, New World for more robust, fruity wines. Whilst partly true, as a wine buyer I'd meet French winemakers in Chile, Chilean winemakers in New Zealand and Australian winemakers in France. Actually, the most obvious difference between the Old World and New World is one you can see rather than taste. It's the way the wines are labelled.

Historically, wines from France, Spain, Italy and other European countries have labelled their wines depending on **place** rather than **grape**, giving top billing on the front labels to the place where the grapes are grown rather than the grape variety. For example, Rioja, Chablis and Gavi are all places; they are wine-producing regions. If you take a look at a wine from Australia, New Zealand, South Africa, Chile or Argentina, you'll find the name of the grape variety writ large on the front label. So it helps if you know your grape varieties and your places. However, there are thousands of different grape varieties and wine regions all over the world. I don't plan to tell you about all of them, but I do want to teach you how to navigate the world wine map with your very own built-in satnav.

Here in the UK, even though vineyard plantings are on the increase, we don't produce very much wine (yet), certainly not enough to go around, so we've always been fairly relaxed about drinking wine from elsewhere in the world. That, and a plethora of places to buy wine – led by supermarkets – has given us choice. Arguably, we've had too much choice, leaving us cowering before a great wall of wine, wishing for a sign to point us in the right direction. Unfortunately, help is not always at hand and we're left to go on label, and previous experience, alone. In which case, it's good to know how to decode a label. Overleaf is what to look for when you pick up a bottle of wine:

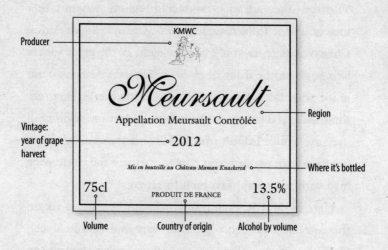

Producer

KMWC

Meursault

Appellation Meursault Contrôlée

2012

Region

Vintage: year of grape harvest

Mis en bouteille au Château Maman Knackered

Where it's bottled

75cl

PRODUIT DE FRANCE

13.5%

Volume

Country of origin

Alcohol by volume

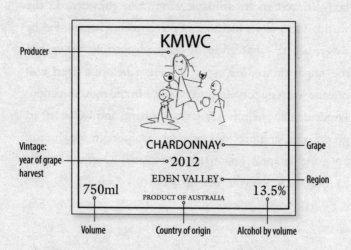

Producer

KMWC

CHARDONNAY

2012

EDEN VALLEY

Grape

Region

Vintage: year of grape harvest

750ml

PRODUCT OF AUSTRALIA

13.5%

Volume

Country of origin

Alcohol by volume

GETTING STARTED

The selection on page 24 of fridge-door whites and in-the-rack reds is based on what I've recently found and loved when that night-time blanket descends. The wines here are likely to be poured before food is on the table in the case of the whites, but drunk with food in the case of the reds. The rosé is for when it's warm enough to sit outside once the children are in bed, with a small bowl of something to nibble at in front of me.

What I would like you to do is write down the country and grape for each wine, take the list to your local shop, whether that's a supermarket, a wine specialist, or an online retailer, and search for some of these wines (look! You're doing homework already – grown-up homework). See what you find. If you can't find the grape listed below, try a different grape or something from another region in the same country at a similar price. Forget the school run; this is the wine run. It's more fun (and there's less shouting).

DEAL OR NO DEAL?

Apparently more than two-thirds of all booze in the UK is bought when it's on offer. I was quite surprised by this. Until I thought about it, that is. I love a bargain. I can't remember the last time I bought baby wipes that weren't on a three-for-two offer. Crisps on buy-one-get-one-free?

Chuck 'em in. Washing powder, bags of apples, packs of mince, tins of tuna . . . Extra points? Lovely. You know the deal.

When it comes to wine, I'll check out the offers before looking at the rest of the wine aisle. The problem is, the choice of wines on offer gets a bit samey, so I urge you to move on from the bargains if you've tried the wines before. If you're in the supermarket, look at the labels, scan for the country, place, grape variety and vintage, read the story on the back label. I know this means slowing down the trolley-dash just a bit, but it's time well spent. Unless you have a small child pulling at your arm, or shouting that they need a wee NOW, in which case all bets are off. Leave it until next time.

Supermarkets aren't known for providing readily available wine experts in the wine aisle, but some are definitely putting more time and effort into doing this. However, it's more likely it will just be you and at least 500 labels to look at, with a few bits of information scattered around on the shelves. This is when you need your wine satnav to kick in (which you'll have by the end of the book). If, however, you are in a specialist wine shop, then ask the person behind the counter what they recommend. Ask them if they have tried it themselves – they probably will have. The people in specialist wine shops, or local independent wine shops are usually abnormally obsessive about wine, so give them an opportunity to help you explore their range and see what happens. The last time I did that in my local wine shop, I left with an Italian red made from a grape I'd never tried (or even heard of) and it was utterly delicious. It is worth asking if you can try it before you buy – you never know, they might be happy to open a bottle if they think others might want to try it. I've given you a price as a guide, but you may have to spend a bit more or a bit less, depending on where you shop.

The idea behind this exercise is to give you a starting point and to get you thinking about wine and being open to trying new things. Think of it as encouraging your defiant child to try something new. Remember all those times you have begged, *pleaded* with them just to taste it. Is there anything more soul-destroying than tipping a plate of uneaten freshly made food into the bin after an emotional teatime? Just as they have the power to make you feel happy when they discover a new taste and go on to wolf it down, so you can make me happy by trying something new. If you don't like it, that's fine. But you need to try it – perhaps a few times – before saying no. Off you go.

Colour?	Style?	Where from?	What grape is it made from?	Why choose it?	Wonga?
White	Crisp	Italy (Campania region)	Falanghina	Dry, refreshing, undemanding but lovely	£7–9
White	Fruity	Chile (Casablanca region)	Viognier	Bright, sunshiney, with pineapple fruit	£8–10
White	Smooth	New Zealand (Gisborne region)	Chardonnay	Ripe, round white, perhaps with a bit of oak	£8–10
Rosé	Cheerful	Spain (Navarra region)	Garnacha	Juicy, lively, easy-drinking	£7–9
Red	Easy-going	France (Beaujolais region)	Gamay	Light, bright and friendly, kinda cool	£7–9
Red	Juicy	Italy (Sicily)	Nero d'Avola	Ripe, juicy, crammed with berry fruit	£7–9
Red	Bold and beautiful	Argentina (Mendoza region)	Malbec	Bit of a show-off but great fun	£7–9

As mentioned, there are thousands of grape varieties grown all over the world. We've started with just a few, but I'm thinking tortoise and hare. We're in it for the long run.

Once you've got a couple of these wines in, you need to taste them. I mean, really give them a good going over as in swirling and swishing. We obviously have to address the issue of spitting versus swallowing (no sniggering at the back, please). A good, clean aim is essential when it comes to professional wine tasting and spitting the wine into a spittoon. Eldest Boy thinks it's hilarious that in my job as a 'wine lady' I have to spit when *everyone* knows spitting is rude. And there's also a no aftershave/perfume/hairspray rule (unwritten) at professional wine tastings, which is probably why I absolutely drench myself Jilly Cooper-heroine-like in perfume when I'm not working and on a night out, even if it's only a parents' evening. However, we're not doing this professionally, so spitting is optional.

Seriously, though, there is an art to tasting wine and we'll look at how to do it properly in the next chapter.

10 THINGS I KNOW ABOUT WINE (AND WANT TO SHARE WITH YOU)

1. New Zealand Pinot Noir is usually divine.

2. Cheap South African red usually isn't.

3. Champagne with a bit of age is much more interesting than young stuff.

4. Chilean Cabernet Sauvignon from the Colchagua region tastes a bit like chocolate.

5. The Nebbiolo grape (of Barolo fame) is an awkward bugger but I still love it.

6. English wines, especially sparkling ones, are getting better with every (good) vintage.

7. We all need to drink more Vermentino.
8. Top-end Burgundy is to die for, really.
9. I thought I always preferred Old World Sauvignon Blanc to New World Sauvignon Blanc, but I was wrong.
10. Left-field is good: Austrian Grüner Veltliner, southern Italian reds, under-the-radar Languedoc regions . . .

CHAPTER
TWO

BACK TO
(WINE) SCHOOL

As much as I can't bear leaving the summer behind, I have to admit to feeling just a tiny bit relieved when the children go back to school. By the end of the holidays, my children look like wild things with their long hair and sun-kissed skin. Not quite Boden-perfect, owing to the vast number of hand-me-downs worn in this house, but you get the picture. I just look even more knackered than usual. Yes, there is joy in not having to be in the car by 8.15 a.m. every morning with three children dressed, fed and ready for school, but the *lack* of routine is almost as exhausting. And there are definitely more tears before bedtime as the late nights take their toll.

So it's with a little inward sigh that I start sewing name tapes onto new school jumpers, or rather scrawl names across labels with a laundry marker pen (from Lakeland, of course). I did do the sewing of name tapes when Eldest Boy started school – I think it's a rite of passage – but then discovered that a laundry pen makes life much simpler. And we like that. So, with the promise of a new school year ahead of us, I thought this would be the perfect moment to go back to wine school and make sure we've got the basics right. Like the three Rs, although I've never understood why they are called that when two of the three Rs don't begin with R. Anyway, stop daydreaming at the back and pay attention.

HOW IS WINE MADE?

This is a bit of a crash course, but here's my guide to how wine is made. Funnily enough, there is more to it than getting some ripe grapes, squashing them, adding yeast and hoping for the best. I know this technique is still employed by many across the land who fancy themselves as a bit of a winemaker (my brother-in-law included), but I have tasted 'Chateau Coach House' and, trust me, it could burn a hole in your throat.

Modern-day winemaking means that winemakers are capable of making the very best from nature's party trick. The main aim when making a wine is to preserve the natural fruit flavours of the grape, and so it follows that really good wine can only be made from really good grapes. White wines are made by picking the grapes, crushing and pressing them to get the juice out, then fermenting them without the skins. This is because all grape juice is clear; it is the skins that give the resulting wine its colour. White wine needs to be made without the skins so the juice stays clear and the resulting wine stays white.

Red wine is made differently. The juice of red grapes is also clear, but letting it ferment with the skins of the grapes gives the juice colour. Red grapes will be crushed and sometimes left to macerate (meaning left in contact) with their skins so the juice can take up more of the colour and tannin from the skins before fermentation.

Some wines are made using natural yeasts, that is, yeasts found on the skin of the grapes. However, this makes the fermentation process a tad unpredictable, so many winemakers now add manufactured yeasts for a little more predictability and to help it along. The juice, skins and yeasts are left to ferment, usually in large stainless-steel tanks or concrete vats and sometimes, for the very brave (due to the cost and slightly less predictable results), in (usually) oak barrels. Fermentation temperatures need to be carefully controlled, ensuring they don't get too hot (when flavours might be lost) or too cold (when fermentation might stop). The juice needs to warm up enough to allow fermentation to happen, which is usually at about 13 degrees or above. The fermentation may take anything from a few days to a few weeks depending on what's being made, and if it's a red wine the skins and juice will be mixed up to ensure the juice takes on the colour of the skins (we'll cover how this is done in more detail later on). Most wines are then filtered and fined (any unwanted bits taken out), ready for bottling. Unless the winemaker has decided to stick it in barrels to age it a bit more, in which case off it goes to do its thing (again, more of that later).

WHAT AFFECTS THE FLAVOUR OF WINE?

OK, winos, you're doing well. Now we'll look at what affects the flavour of a wine. Whereas the ingredients list for wine is incredibly short, the list of things that can affect the flavour of a wine is not. These include 1) the grape variety, 2) where it's grown, 3) how it's grown and 4) who made it. All these things will determine the end flavour. Starting with the grape variety, we're not talking baked beans. There are a lot more than fifty-seven varieties. There are thousands, in fact. Styles can vary from very aromatic to downright dull. They can produce huge bunches of big, juicy grapes or tight little bunches of tiny grapes. And the colour of the grapes can vary from the palest yellow to inky black.

Where the vine is grown affects how the grape will grow. There are vineyards that lie close to the sea, brushed over daily by sea breezes, then there are the picture-perfect vineyards that lie on gently sloping hills, like those in the Côte d'Or in Burgundy (where one day I shall retire, drink Pinot Noir and eat stinky cheese for breakfast if I so wish). More dramatically, there are vineyards that nestle in the foothills of mountain ranges, as in Chile and Argentina. Grapes need about 1,500 hours of sunshine to ripen, black grapes needing a bit more than white. The upside of climate change is that it's getting easier to grow grapes and ripen them enough to make wine in England. Admittedly that doesn't quite balance with the cons, but it's an upside nonetheless.

If a vineyard is near the sea or high up in mountain foothills, the cooler air will slow down the ripening process, allowing the grape to develop distinctive varietal characters. If a grape ripens too quickly, the end result may be a wine with lots of alcohol but not enough acidity. You'll learn why that's not a good thing in a moment.

This is all good practical stuff. Talking of which, for my last birthday I wrote a present wish list. It looked like this:

1. A wheelbarrow
2. A new roasting dish

That was it. Pathetic. In years gone by, the lists started *months* before the birthday. It was full of desirable, mostly shallow items, with a few books thrown in to make me look clever. And now? My life was not complete until I got that wheelbarrow (which I did, as it happens). Anyway, the point is, I think we reach a stage in our lives when the frivolous stuff is great, but the practical stuff is better. You've just worked your way through quite a chunk of practical information about wine. It might not be as helpful as a pot of Crème de la Mer, but this book didn't cost you over a hundred quid and we all get wrinkles in the end, so clever you.

WHAT IS *TERROIR?*

This is a French word with no direct translation. The best I can do is 'soil' but that doesn't do it, really. *Terroir* is a reference to the actual place where a grape is grown, the combination of soil, aspect of the vineyards and climatic conditions. In fact, everything outside of the winemaker's control is one way – OK, my way – to think of it. It can't be easily defined in a word as it's a combination of factors, so it's not a word you'll find on the label. However, some wines do use the name of a distinctive character such as silex (a type of soil found in the Sancerre region) on the label.

✳ RULES RULE, OK?

Tradition is a big thing in wine. Over time, traditions develop for seemingly no other reason than the fact that this is how it's always been done. Look at morris dancing: same principle. Wine traditions have shaped what variety is grown where and how a particular wine from a particular region must be made, down to how many grapes can be taken from the vine to make wine, time spent ageing in oak barrels and what goes on the labels. This is largely an Old World thing, resulting in rules and regulations being put in place to protect these traditions. In France, the *appellation d'origine controlée* system works to do just that. Spain, Italy and most other European wine-producing countries have their own rules and regulations, and now the rest of the world is following suit. Rules can be good when it comes to enforcing, or rather protecting, wine quality. If you see the letters AC (for French wine), DO (for Spanish) or DOC (for Italian wine) on the label, it tells you that the wine has been made according to the traditions and rules of a particular region.

Finally, there is the way the wine is made, what the winemakers do to it. Depending on where it is made and what is allowed according to local rules, they might put it into oak barrels, or add some sugar to it, or even take some alcohol out of it, and all of these things will affect the flavour.

HOW DO YOU TASTE WINE?

I do a lot of wine tasting as part of my job. This involves both vertical tastings (wines from the same producer but made in different vintages) and horizontal tastings (wines from different producers in the same region from the same year), although a horizontal tasting after hours usually involves a sofa rather than writing tasting notes. Even when tasting professionally, I employ the same approach as I do at home, namely: look, smell, taste.

It sounds perfectly straightforward, but how many times

do you pick up a glass and just take a sip without giving the smell much thought? If you do take a slug without swilling and sniffing the wine, you miss out on about two-thirds of what that wine has to offer. This is because tasting a wine is actually more about smelling it than tasting it.

But before you sniff, open your eyes and look at what's in your glass, which is hopefully something from the list in the first chapter.

✳ LOOK

The first thing to do is look at it. Really look at it, properly, against a white background if possible, so you can see the colour as clearly as possible. For white wine, think about the colour: is it pale yellow or straw-coloured? The darker it is, the older it might be. For red, it's the other way round, with garnet or brick-coloured reds usually being older than the inky-black young guns.

Make sure your glass is less than half full, ideally about a third full in fact, and give it a really good swirl to release the aromas. If you happen to have a small, tulip-shaped wine glass, then you've got a perfectly shaped glass for tasting, unless it is tinted pink (in which case save those for when you're next on *Come Dine With Me*). Otherwise, any normal-sized wine glass will do, as long as it's a) really clean and free of any soapy scents and b) not more than a third full.

✳ SMELL

Next, swill it around, shove your nose right in the glass and take a good, long sniff. By doing this, you are giving the hundreds of receptors inside your nose the opportunity to do their thing and send messages to the brain about what it is you're smelling, be it citrus fruits, black fruits, red fruits, spice, oak or whatever else you might find in there. As you sniff, your brain is flicking through a Rolodex of listed descriptors, trying to recognize what's in the glass. That's why it's worth spending a bit of time building up your flavour contacts so that you can adequately describe it, even if it's just mentally, to yourself.

Best not to be drenched in Diorissimo when doing this. The same goes for hairspray.

✳ TASTE

Finally, take a small amount of wine in your mouth and swill it around, preferably pulling in a little bit of air at the same time. If you have no idea what I'm on about, have a look at the video I've done on the blog called, imaginatively, 'How to taste wine' (and apologies for the wink to camera; I've no idea why I do this).

It takes time and dedicated practice not to look ridiculous whilst doing this, so don't be surprised if your first attempt results in spitting the wine out over the person sitting opposite you. In fact, probably wise not to attempt this for the first time when sitting opposite someone, unless you don't like them much.

Purse your lips, suck in air through a tiny hole and knock the wine around the mouth. Coat the tongue, gums, back of the mouth and let your taste buds (you've got about 10,000 of them) on your tongue get their fill. Think about the fruit flavours, the zip (aka 'acidity'), the grip (aka 'tannins'), the oomph (aka 'body') and the balance and structure, all of which I'll explain in a bit more detail in the next bit. Of course, you don't have to think about any of those things, just decide whether you like it or not, but taking the time to taste a wine properly like this does make a huge difference to how you'll feel about the wine afterwards and also how you'll remember it.

You don't have to do this almost ceremonial act every time you take a sip – it makes a fairly unattractive noise and you risk looking a bit weird – but it's definitely worth doing if you want to get properly acquainted with the wine.

HOW DO YOU DESCRIBE WINE?

Wine is often described with specific words and some general face-pulling and arm-waving, even by the experts. The 'expert' dictionary includes words like structure, weight, balance and mouth-feel, giving us a framework to describe a wine and assess its quality. For example, a wine might be described as having great structure, with balance. What this means is that the components of the wine – fruit, sugar, alcohol and tannin – work well together; they are balanced, one single component doesn't shout over another. Even though you don't need to know the full dictionary of words, it's useful to have an understanding of some of these terms so that you can describe what it is you are tasting beyond just the fruit characteristics. Here's a guide to what some of the most commonly used 'winey' words mean (warning: they sound quite poncey):

Wine word	What does it mean?
Structure	How the components of a wine come together (fruit, sugar, alcohol, tannin) and affect the overall balance of a wine
Body	This is mostly to do with alcohol and sugar, but is a reference to how it feels in the mouth, i.e., full-bodied or light-bodied? Think skimmed milk versus full-fat milk. Not the taste, obviously, but the weight of it in your mouth. Very different
Balance	A way of describing how the different parts – alcohol, sweetness, acidity and tannins – sit together in the wine
Tannin	The 'grip' of a wine, determined by how much tannin (see previous chapter) has been extracted from the grapes (and sometimes oak) into the wine

✳ BODY (NOT MINE): LIGHT-BODIED, MEDIUM-BODIED OR FULL-BODIED?

I don't go out that often nowadays, but when I do I make the most of it. Especially when there's dancing. The problem is, on the night I am born to dance; the next day I can't walk properly. Turns out, the hips do lie (I'm talking to *you*, Shakira). My body slopes around, leaving me trapped inside shouting, 'THIS NEVER USED TO HAPPEN! THIS IS NOT MY BODY!' But the evidence seems to suggest otherwise, dammit.

Anyway, wine is often described in terms of body, specifically being light-, medium- or full-bodied. A bit like milk: skimmed being light, semi-skimmed being medium and full-fat being full-bodied. But in truth what is full-bodied to you might feel medium-bodied to someone who likes big, robust wines. It's all a matter of individual taste. However, having some sort of guide helps when choosing wine. Here's a body map, slightly less ravaged than mine:

* **Light-bodied:** a light white wine; an easy-going red wine with soft tannins such as Beaujolais; a light-coloured rosé wine; most sparkling wines.
* **Medium-bodied:** a fruity white, perhaps with a bit of oak; a weightier red wine, but still not too heavy on the tannins; a very pink rosé.
* **Full-bodied:** a rich, sweet white or a big, oaky white; a rich, spicy red, most likely with oak; a vintage Champagne.

✳ FEELING FRUITY

As well as these more technical terms, wine is also described on back labels by the fruit characters they might have. For example, is the wine fruity? If so, is it black fruits or red fruits? Is it citrus or tropical fruit? Is it perhaps more vegetal than fruity, say herby or grassy? It might even be more floral than fruity, something like orange blossom or jasmine? With red wine, you may find fruit but also more woody aromas, or spice such as cinnamon. The combination is endless and fascinating.

The problem is, sometimes the label might tell you one thing, but your nose and taste buds find another. That's fine, don't get too stuck on what you 'should' be finding in your glass. Just enjoy it for what you find. Often, I've got my nose in a glass and there's something I can smell but I just can't put my finger on it. Then the second someone says what it is, it's almost as if I can smell it even more. Equally, when a label tells me I'm going to find liquorice in a wine I approach with caution: I can't bear liquorice. As a child, I remember eating the pink coconut surrounding from Liquorice Allsorts and sneaking the dreaded black middle bit back into the bag. Luckily, most of the time in wine it's more of a whiff, a trace of liquorice rather than a taste. As a guide, overleaf is a simple 'nose guide' that points to the main groups found in wine.

✳ TAKE THIS DOWN

I live my life by lists. This is for a number of reasons, mostly because with every child that I've had, I seem to have lost the capacity to remember stuff. I wouldn't even contemplate going into a supermarket nowadays without a scribbled list of what I need. If I don't have one I come out with more yoghurts, a birthday card and some on-offer chocolate ice cream, but nothing for us to actually eat that night. When it comes to remembering things about wine, I have learnt

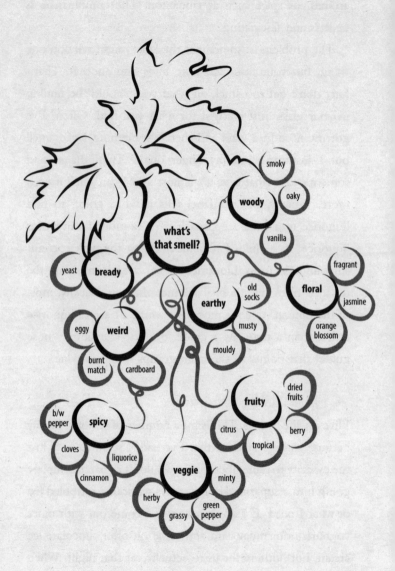

to scribble down just a few words that will trigger a memory about it. A few key pointers – bright, vibrant, juicy, crisp – that will remind me if I liked it or not. Here are some of my recent tasting notes from a wine competition I took part in recently, just to give you an idea of the sort of pointers I use when tasting professionally:

* **Unidentified Italian Fiano (white):** clean, fresh nose with lemon peel notes. Crisp and fresh on the palate, nicely balanced fruit and acidity, hit of citrus fruit on the finish.
* **Unidentified Australian Grenache (red):** clean, vibrant redcurrant aromas, bright and juicy with fleshy red fruits on the palate. Medium-weight with well-structured tannins, integrated oak and kick of spice on the finish.

Not the most exciting tasting notes and certainly not back-label friendly, as they don't tell you anything about where the wine came from and who made it, but when tasting professionally my job is to assess the balance of the wines, to see if they 'work' or not. When writing tasting notes for wine is your day job, it doesn't feel remotely strange doing this, but if you've never written a tasting note in your life, you probably won't know where to start. If this is the case, I suggest you begin with a simple star or tick system: one star is OK, three stars is pretty good, five stars means you'll buy it again. No stars equals thanks but no thanks.

As you get comfortable with rating a wine (and remember, no one but you can say if you like it or not, and if so, how much), then try and note down a few words that describe it. Not just fruit, floral or vegetal descriptors, but words that describe the style of the wine. Is it fresh? Is it juicy? Is it brooding (by which I mean, is it a smouldering red, all rustic and grrrrrr, a bit of an animal)? Write it in a notebook (it's a good excuse to buy a swanky notebook, if nothing else), or put a note in your phone. It doesn't matter. Just write it and start to build up your own little scribbled list of wines you like and wines you don't. Of course, this only works if you're trying new things. But you've already signed up to do that, so we're good. Keep your list in your bag, so that next time you're shopping you will hopefully spend less time staring, baffled, at the wall of wine, and more time selecting new wines based on your notes, while feeling ever-so-slightly smug and rather grown-up. Here are some wine-tasting notes done by fellow knackered mothers, when asked what they thought about wines:

* **A dry, aromatic Hungarian Gewürztraminer (white):**
    * 'Really quite delicious, very quaffable wine that matches perfectly with spicy food, or indeed, and rather randomly, cheese.'

* 'Not usually a fan of fruity wines but this is very drinkable. Can imagine drinking on a warm, sunny weekend afternoon, in the sun. Not really that dry, smells sweeter than it tastes.'

* 'Yummy, delicious floral-tasting wine that chased away the grumpy taste left by my husband!'

* **A bold, fruity Argentinian Malbec (red):**

  * 'Fruity, brash and upfront, very drinkable party wine.'

  * 'Full-bodied, fruity, blackberries, warm and rich.'

  * 'Nice fruity smells, bold first taste, fruity and spicy at the end.'

  * 'Yummy!'

  * 'It's reeeally dark and strong (don't know technical term for that). And there's something fruity – really dark black cherries or . . . and don't laugh . . . blue-berries? Although I have been eating blueberries today, so maybe they're just stuck in my teeth. Ha ha.'

The point is they're the same wines, different reactions. There is no right or wrong, just say (or write) what you see, smell and taste. Only you know if you like a wine or not, no matter how special/expensive someone tells you it is. Just scribble that note and concentrate on building your own personal wine satnav.

✳ THE SHAPE OF WINE TO COME

Having just told you to make a brief note about a wine if you are trying it for the first time, I have to tell you about my friend Joe. He knows a lot about wine. His father was a chef, he lived in and around hotels growing up and he lives and breathes wine. Literally. He has an amazing palate. Joe also has an encyclopedic mind; he's the one you want on your pub-quiz team. But what I find really amazing about him is that in all the years I've spent writing tasting notes for wines as part of my job, Joe has never written a single one. This is partly due to that incredible memory of his, but he's also got a very short attention span. Writing endless tasting notes is simply not for him. Consequently, he has developed a skill for remembering wines not just because of how they taste, but because of their shape.

I know this sounds a bit contrived, but when you think about it, wine does have form. There are ripe, round wines that fill the whole of the mouth and seduce the taste buds, and there are sharp, angular wines with crisp edges and flavours. He once described a wine as akin to having a piece of Lego in your mouth, and I knew exactly what he meant (not that I make a habit of putting Lego in my mouth). Thinking of these wines as shapes or forms rather than 'Does this taste of apples?' is a really good way of looking at it.

WHAT TEMPERATURE TO TASTE WINE?

Often, the back label will tell you to serve a red wine at room temperature and a white wine chilled. However, I'm guessing room temperature in your average grand French chateau is probably a little cooler than my sitting room. Not that I make a habit of taking the temperature of a wine on serving (although there are plenty of gadgets for sale that do this, usually targeted at those with more money than sense), but as a guide, 18 degrees is about the warmest you want to drink a red, any warmer and it will feel like soup. My father-in-law went through a phase of warming red wine up in the microwave. It was a cold house, granted, but even so I don't recommend doing this unless you want your red wine lukewarm. For white, go for about 8 degrees on sparklers and a little less chilled (about 10 degrees) for whites. Too cold and the aromas will struggle to make an impact and the flavours will be muted. Again, use common sense. If a white wine feels too cold, leave it on the side and come back in half an hour. If it's too warm, stick it in the freezer for twenty minutes (set the oven timer so you don't forget it).

With red, go for about 14 degrees, even a little chilled in the summer. The French have a long tradition of serving some of their lighter red wines, particularly those from Beaujolais, slightly chilled. The reason for doing this is that temperature affects the way wine feels in the mouth. Cooler temperatures can make the tannins feel more prominent and the alcohol less so. Hence, lighter-bodied red wines with soft tannins can feel a little more robust if slightly chilled.

So, a lot of information, but that internal wine satnav is being loaded up nicely. Now, it's party time.

CHAPTER

THREE

PARTY TIME

We go to a lot of parties, mostly on yachts, in beautiful villas and at secluded chalets in the mountains. I used to get fazed by all the beautiful people and occasional celebs, but now some of them are my best friends. They're just so *normal*.

OK, I lie. The majority of the parties I go to these days involve hot dogs and a cake at a friend's house. Yes, our lives are governed by children's parties rather than ones for grown-ups, though we do still throw the odd grown-up one. Take our housewarming; after years of renting, we finally moved into a 1970s-built bungalow in the woods. It has a whiff of *The Ice Storm* about it, but without the swinging (don't let that put you off if you haven't seen the film, it's brilliant). In fact, a few of the houses do have pampas grass outside, so it was with a tiny niggle of trepidation that we invited all of our neighbours in for a drink just before Christmas. I'm happy to report that said niggle was needless and the party went with a bang (without the gang).

Then there's the art of throwing a good children's party. With Eldest Boy we went completely over the top for his first birthday. We ended up joining forces with about five other couples (friends seem to breed in batches, have you noticed?) and had a big picnic in a London park with lots of cake, sandwiches and a bucket of Pimm's. The next few years saw cakes made in the shape of trains, magicians booked and plenty of bunting. Then the penny dropped. All they really want is you, a cake, some balloons, a few friends and family and to do well on the present front. Consequently, Middle Boy got his first proper party at three years old and Youngest Girl was the same.

Whether throwing a party for three or thirty, the essential ingredients don't vary much. My default was always sandwiches (egg, marmite or jam), bacon flavour crisps, mini sausages, carrot sticks (mostly untouched, but at least it shows the other parents that you're on it when it comes to five a day). And, of course, a giant chocolate cake covered in chocolate icing and Smarties/pink icing and butterfly sprinkles (this isn't enforced genderization, it's what they ask for, I *swear*).

I do have a friend who makes the most amazing cakes. We're talking fairy princess castles, racing tracks, football pitches. I am in awe, but I'm not even going to try. It would end in tears. The train cake was a boundary pusher for me and the result was at least edible, even if it didn't really look much like the picture. More of a train crash, really. I threw Jelly Tots at it and no one seemed to mind, least of all Eldest Boy.

Then there was a spate of christenings and naming days to attend, although sadly these are tailing off now. In fact, such was our run of christenings that our local vicar asked me to write a wine column for the parish magazine on the grounds that I only ever turned up at church to get another child christened. He had a point.

It's all landmark birthdays and wedding anniversaries from here on in. In fact, talking of wedding anniversaries, we went to Venice for our tenth anniversary. There was much excitement all round, not least because the children seemed to sense the highly indulgent grandparenting that lay ahead. I thought I'd buy something new for the occasion. What do you think that might have been: underwear that actually matched, perhaps? A springtastic print scarf? Flatforms to make it clear I still read *Vogue* and know what Alexa Chung is wearing? Don't be ridiculous. Said purchase was a deeply unattractive back support belt for moderate back pain, owing to a knackered sacroiliac joint brought on by carrying babies. Not the look I was going for on the big anniversary trip. In Venice. Where you have to walk everywhere. Hey ho.

Throwing a party – especially a children's party – brings with it a certain amount of stress. The last thing you need is to worry about looking after the adults of children who come to the party. There is a simple way to bring them together so they can take care of themselves, and that is by providing a small glass of something with bubbles in it to make up for the fact that they are having to spend their Saturday afternoon at a noisy children's party when they'd probably rather be somewhere else, if they were completely honest. Of course, there are lots of people who are genuinely happy to be there – I'm thinking of grandparents – but you don't have to worry about them. So, let's talk fizz.

WHAT MAKES WINE BUBBLY?

Before we get on to what type of fizz to serve, let's have a look at what makes a wine sparkle. Here comes the science part, as they say (or at least Jennifer Aniston did once, in a hair commercial. I found it very irritating, so I'm not sure why I've used it. Apologies).

There are a number of ways to get those bubbles in a bottle. The traditional – and most expensive – method is by adding a bit more yeast to wine in a bottle, sealing it and letting it undergo a second fermentation in the bottle. This double fermentation process creates tiny bubbles (CO_2) and if the bottle is sealed then obviously the bubbles can't escape. Instead, they stay in the wine, adding sparkle. Champagne is made this way, along with other sparkling wines around the world, including Cava. If made this way, the dead yeast cells, called lees, need to be removed from the bottle before it's sold. This is done by riddling (slowly moving the bottles by hand or machine) so that the lees end up collecting in the top of the bottle. The tops of the bottles are then frozen and the ice cube containing the lees is popped out, the bottles topped up with the desired sugar dose (or 'dosage' as it's known in Champagne) and resealed. Hence the price.

Another, cheaper way to make sparkling wine is to do the second fermentation in a tank and then bottle the wine under pressure to keep the bubbles. This is known as the 'tank method' or Charmat method, named after the man who invented it. This is how Prosecco is made, accounting for the softer bubbles (and cheaper production costs). Then there's the bicycle-pump method (the technical term is carbonation, but I prefer bicycle pump), the premise being that you get a tank full of wine and pump bubbles into it. The end result is fairly coarse, big bubbles that dissipate quickly, but bubbles nonetheless. This method is used to make cheap – and sometimes not very cheerful – sparkling wines.

When it comes to choosing sparkling wines (indeed any wines) for a crowd of people without it costing the earth, you need to do a bit of research. Do an online trawl to see what's on offer at various supermarkets, wine specialists and your local wine merchant, and sign up for e-newsletters whilst you're there (they're a brilliant way to get advance warning when a good offer comes along; essential when buying in bulk). But to save yourself time and money, it helps if you know what you're looking for. Here are the main types of wine with bubbles:

Name	Where is it made?	What grapes is it made from?	What style is it?	Good for parties?	How much?
Cava	Spain (mostly in the Penedès region)	A blend of some or all Xarel-lo, Parellada, Macabeo, Chardonnay	Usually dry or off-dry and fruity	A bit hit-and-miss, but find a good one, especially vintage, and you're laughing	From £6–15
Champagne	France (Champagne region)	A blend of some or all Chardonnay, Pinot Meunier, Pinot Noir	Sharper than Cava, more serious	More expensive, but worth it if you want a classic fizz	From £20–40 with a few (drinkable) cheaper ones to be found
Crémant	France (Loire, Alsace, Bourgogne, Jura, Bordeaux, Limoux)	Made in the same way as champagne, often from the same grape varieties, but from regions other than Champagne	Similar to Champagne but sometimes more fruity	Brilliant – looks like Champagne, tastes a bit like Champagne but usually half the price	£10–20
Prosecco	Italy (Veneto region)	Glera (usually called Prosecco)	Light, easy-going, simple	Brilliant for parties, especially daytime ones	About £10–15
Other traditional method sparkling wines	Australia, South Africa, New Zealand, Chile, Argentina, England	Often use traditional Champagne grapes but can be anything!	Usually dry, crisp, fruity and good value	Much more variable, but good ones can be perfect for parties	£12–30, as price depends on where it's from

A note on quantities: it's always better to overcater than run out. Wine keeps, not for ever but longer than sausage rolls for sure. When calculating quantities for children's parties, you need to allow for a glass per person, as some will be driving. Work on six glasses per bottle.

Whilst we're on quantities, I am often asked about how much to buy for weddings. I usually work on half a bottle per person, plus a few extra cases on top, just in case. Again, with some people driving and some compensating, this usually covers it. At our own wedding, my father was very impressed with his carefully worked out quantity calculations, as we only had four bottles of Champagne left at the end. What he didn't know was that my brother was last seen at 2 a.m., loading a car up with all the leftover full cases before disappearing off to finish it with friends in a nearby barn. Apparently it was quite an after-party.

FULL ENGLISH?

Rumour has it that English sparkling wines are as good as Champagne nowadays. Do I think that's true? Well, certainly in terms of climate, we're not far off, with similar temperatures and rainfall. And the chalky soils of the North and South Downs, where many English vineyards are found, are not a million miles away from those of Champagne. In fact, less than a hundred miles lies between some of them. Many vineyards are now planted with the same grapes that make great Champagne, namely Chardonnay, Pinot Noir and Pinot Meunier.

Certainly the quality of English sparkling wines has come a long way in the last twenty years. The best wines are certainly comparable to Champagne but with their own distinctive character, as they should. As yet, most English sparkling wines remain expensive by comparison, largely due to the smaller-scale production. Having said that, the number of vineyards have more than doubled over the last decade and the future looks bright. And bubbly, with some seriously good still wines too. Some names to look out for include Ridgeview, Nyetimber, Chapel Down, Wiston, Camel Valley, Gusbourne, Hambledon, Bolney and Breaky Bottom (I didn't make the last one up).

CROWD PLEASERS

If you're getting in reds and whites for a party, think about whether they will be served with hearty food or just nibbles. If we're talking cheese straws and peanuts, then keep the white wine light-bodied, crisp and fruity. For reds, stick to easy-going. If you're going to the trouble of making food to feed the crowd, then it's a good idea to put a bit of thought into which wines might best complement it.

We're coming on to matching food and wine later in the book, but for the cheese-straw-and-peanut party, then Spain, Chile and South Africa are all great places to look for great-value wines that please a crowd. The generally soft, fruity style of the wines is ideal: a white blend for the white and Merlot for the red is tried and tested. Try before you buy if at all possible, as there are always anomalies. But generally, when you need to buy for a crowd and keep to a budget, these countries don't let me down when it comes to great-value party wines. I don't want you to think I am suggesting you go for unadventurous wines, more that it makes sense to serve wines that are reliable, generally liked and obviously not too expensive when catering for large numbers. Here are some pointers for crowd-pleasing wine-and-nibble combos:

Nibble of choice	Suggested wine	What style is it?
Cheese straws and nuts	Spanish Verdejo	Ripe, round and easy-going
Egg and cress sandwiches	Cava	Crisp, bubbly and citrusy
Plate of cheeses	Chilean Merlot	Soft, juicy and mellow
Crudités	French Picpoul	Lively, fresh and lemony
Blinis	New Zealand Sauvignon Blanc	Zesty, bright and crisp
Sausage rolls	Spanish Tempranillo	Smooth, juicy and uncomplicated
Fairy cakes	Prosecco	Frothy, light and delicate

PACKING A PUNCH

There is another way. You could put on your housecoat and go retro with a party punch. I'm being serious. Punch is a brilliant way to water guests without it costing too much, as well as avoiding any worries you might have about serving wine people might not like (although the fact that you are giving them free drinks means they shouldn't be complaining). A huge bowl of party punch for the grown-ups adds a certain *je ne sais quoi* to proceedings, in my experience.

Here's a fallback party punch that has never, ever failed

to keep guests happy. Take a very chilled bottle of Moscato d'Asti (cheap and cheerful Italian sparkling white wine with a fair amount of sweetness) and empty it into a pitcher. Squeeze at least four limes into it, more if you want it really zingy, and stir. Serve straight away. Tastes especially great served in Hello Kitty paper cups.

One more suggestion, if only bubbles will do, is sparkling cider. There are some brilliant bottle-fermented sparkling ciders around. Gospel Green (made in Sussex) is one I know and love, introduced to me by one of my book-club friends, Swallow (not her real name, but you'll hear more about that later). At 8.5 per cent, it's light, bubbly, appley and delicious. Or if you want something a little like Prosecco but perhaps not as sweet, try Pignoletto. It comes from the Emilia Romagna region in Italy and is made in the same way as Prosecco but from the Pignoletto grape. Makes a properly refreshing change.

TRUE OR FALSE: SULPHUR IN WINES CAUSES A HANGOVER

Sulphur is used in winemaking as a tool to keep air away from the unfermented grape juice and resulting wine, so the liquid in question won't oxidize. Think of the flesh of an apple, freshly bitten into. Leave it on the side for a while and when you come back to take another bite the flesh has started to go brown. This is because oxygen has got to it and the flesh has oxidized.

Sulphur acts as a barrier to oxygen and means the wine is kept fresh and not exposed to the risk of oxidation. It's also fairly common nowadays to hear sulphur blamed for causing headaches, but the levels found are so very low it's unlikely to be the culprit in most cases. (Unless you're allergic to sulphites of course, in which case stick to wines made with no added sulphur.) Open a pack of dried apricots and there's more than forty times more sulphur in there than in a glass of wine. And did a handful of apricots ever make you feel terrible the next morning? If not, it's more likely the reason for that headache is drinking wine without eating enough food or imbibing enough water at the same time.

Having said that, there has been research to link headaches with levels of naturally occurring histamines in wine, but again this is far from substantiated. So, it's probably not the sulphur that's giving you the headache. It's the wine. The secret is to drink lots of water and eat food (but perhaps not apricots).

If there's one more thing I can throw in here, it's a call to lose the party bags at kids' parties. In fact, let's make a pact: no more party bags. Now *that's* liberating. Time to pick up the last of the Iced Gems (bottom part only) off the floor and head, glass in hand, for the fireside.

CHAPTER

FOUR

FIRESIDE REDS

love winter. In fact, I have the opposite of SAD. In winter I am happy for the following reasons:

1. I can wear big jumpers.
2. I don't have to depilate (such an odd word) for months.
3. The weekend papers aren't full of endless articles about 'festival wear'.
4. We can all put in more TV hours (children and grown-ups alike).
5. I love a salad, but not as much as a big plate of beef stew.
6. I can drink more red wine.

The last point is the one I'm going to talk about here, but first there's something about winter months and depilation that I need to get off my chest. I've got brown hair. Not on my chest, on my head. I don't really give K-Mid a run for her money in the glossy-mane stakes, but I do make an effort and have a little help nowadays to keep the greys at bay. Pre-children, I used to spend a small fortune on waxing, threading and tweezing away hairs in places I didn't want them. But, now that I'm a time-poor, part-time-working, full-time-knackered mother, gone are the salon appointments of yesteryear. Nowadays it's DIY all the way. Luckily, after childbirth, using an epilator on the legs is a relatively painless exercise, but still.

This low-maintenance approach is fine in the winter months when it's only the visible-outside-clothing parts you need to think about (unless you are confident enough to carry off the hirsute look, Julia Roberts-style, when a winning smile helps). That is until you get an invitation to a child's swimming party at the local leisure centre. In November. Which leads to a morning of emergency epilating and a splash of self-loathing about having to hang out in a swimsuit in a pool full of people you might not know very well. So, even though I know it's about the children and not me, for the record I'm not coming in next time.

Anyway, as I was saying, there is something about being inside, knowing that baby, it's cold outside, with the children in bed and the fire lit. Actually, we haven't got an open fire in the *Ice Storm* house. In fact, our small gas fire doesn't even work at the moment. But that doesn't matter if, as we've established, it's cold outside, you're warm inside and you have a gorgeous glass of red in front of you. In fact, it goes hand in hand with curling up and, a bit like hedgehogs, loading up on the food and drink to last us through until the weather gets warmer and the days lighter. There is a heartiness about red wine that white wine just doesn't have.

As you know, the red winemaking process goes like this:

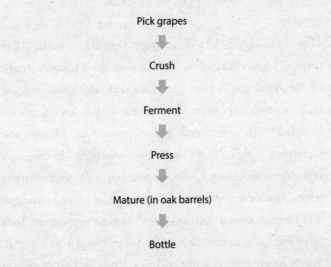

Pick grapes

⬇

Crush

⬇

Ferment

⬇

Press

⬇

Mature (in oak barrels)

⬇

Bottle

Unlike white wine, red wine has masses of colour and tannin. And because all the different grape varieties differ slightly in original colour, size and thickness of skin, calling it simply 'red' wine is a bit like calling all shoes 'shoes' – from Louboutins to FitFlops – when as we know, there's a huge difference. Red wine is actually purple, garnet, inky black, light red, dark red, ruby red, maroon: all colours on the red spectrum.

Now you just have to choose which red wine you want to snuggle up with. As mentioned, there are thousands of varieties, styles and places to choose from, but we're going to start with a bunch of grapes that you need to know about.

CABERNET SAUVIGNON

This is the biggie: like most grape varieties nowadays, this can be found everywhere, but it is as the backbone grape of the Bordeaux region that Cabernet Sauvignon has the right to feel important. In Bordeaux it is almost always blended with other red grapes, including Merlot and Cabernet Franc, but in many southern hemisphere countries, including Chile, it is made as a single variety wine. Almost every bottle containing Cabernet Sauvignon will have the word 'blackcurrant' somewhere on the back label but, as a description, that doesn't begin to cover it. You'll often find all sorts of black fruits in there, such as plums, cherries or berries. IMHO, there is something rather stand-offish about Cabernet Sauvignon, just because it *knows* how good it is. But – *tiny voice* – it is often better blended with other red grapes to make it just a bit softer and more drinkable.

PINOT NOIR

This is a beauty of a grape to drink once it has been made into wine. However, almost as a reminder that she's in charge, Mother Nature ensures that it's not always easy to grow. Pinot Noir vines don't produce abundant crops, as the thin-skinned grapes can't bear cold weather, rain or too much heat (fussy little things).

This grape, which originally comes from Burgundy in France, is responsible for the great wines of the Côte d'Or. It's also shaking its tail feather in New Zealand nowadays, particularly in the South Island in a region called Central Otago. Germany is also raising eyebrows in the wine world with the quality of its Pinot Noir. Rarely cheap but usually good, this is a grape variety to fall in love with over time.

MERLOT

Merlot is a really good grape to have around. On its own, it can produce something gorgeous, but it's usually when it's teamed up with a partner, particularly Cabernet Sauvignon, that it really sings. The fleshy character of Merlot complements the harder backbone of Cabernet Sauvignon, and sometimes the sum is indeed better than the parts. Widely planted across most wine-producing countries, this is fairly easy to grow, ripen and make. It produces soft, lovable wines, hence its popularity the world over. The fact that the variety name is only six letters long and easy enough to say may have helped tbh.

SHIRAZ

So-called in Australia, known as Syrah in France, this is a punchy red grape that gives good fruit. The great red wines of the Rhône Valley are made from Syrah and often described as rich and peppery. I get that, but you can add chocolate to the list too. When chocolate is used in a tasting note, it doesn't mean actual chocolate, obviously. Rather, it means that the aromas might smell a bit like chocolate. Australia's Barossa Valley has made a mark with its Shiraz wines, bold and beautiful with lots of flavour, tannin and alcohol. Not for the faint-hearted, this one. Some people make a sparkling red wine from Shiraz and rave about it. I think emperor's new clothes but am waiting to be proved wrong.

TEMPRANILLO

This red grape is the key ingredient for Rioja wines. It's a great little grape, producing gorgeous cherry-flavoured wines. On its own the wines can be light, fruity and fresh but ultimately forgettable. But put it in an oak barrel and things really start to get interesting. In Rioja, the wines are often aged in American oak barrels, imparting a sweet, vanilla-like flavour to the wine. However, lots of producers are now using French oak barrels, making a more restrained but ultimately richer style of wine.

MALBEC

Argentina is making all the noise about Malbec, but it's also the grape behind Cahors in France, many a holidaymaker's discovery. It is also one of the permitted red grapes grown in Bordeaux, but much of it has been replaced with the more fashionable Cabernet Sauvignon or Merlot grapes. So how to define Malbec? A gatecrasher: late to the party but guaranteed to liven things up. It shakes the taste buds from their noble red grape slumber and says, 'LOOK AT ME! I AM MALBEC AND I. AM. GREAT.' I do love it, though.

ZINFANDEL

California put Zinfandel on the map, but not as a red wine alone. Vast amounts of sweet white wine made from Zinfandel and called 'Blush' is always found in the kitchen at parties at 2 a.m. when everything else has gone.

In its red incarnation, Zinfandel makes a big red wine, with lots of flavour and alcohol. In Italy, Zinfandel's relative is called Primitivo and produces a similar style, but a little more rustic and with the sound turned down – definitely one to try if you haven't already.

* * *

So, I could say, 'Right, these are some of the main grape varieties, learn them by heart and off you go.' But a) I can't think of a good acronym for them and b) all we've done here is have a look at some of the most commonly-found-on-our-shelves grapes so that you can load them into your satnav. What we're going to do now is have a look at a handful of fireside-friendly wine styles from different places. They might not deliver world peace, but they sure do soothe the soul on a cold winter's night, especially if served with a mighty dish of stew. Even better, they are usually properly good value as they aren't the obvious big names. These are my hidden gems, not always easy to find, but if you ask/do a quick bit of research online you will find them, I promise. And it is absolutely worth the effort. All of the wines listed on the following few pages are very winter-food friendly, in fact, they taste much better with food than without.

SOUTHERN ITALIAN REDS FROM THE PUGLIA REGION

Look for wines made from the Primitivo, Negroamaro or Malvasia grapes (found in Salice Salentino wines from Puglia). These are all warm, black, fruit-loaded reds with alcohol levels that let you know they are there. They'll make you want to eat sausage and mash and watch telly.

SOUTHERN FRENCH REDS FROM THE LANGUEDOC REGION

This is a region rich with fireside-friendly red wines. My favourites are almost always a blend of red grapes, including Grenache, Syrah and Mourvèdre, rather than made from one single grape variety. Look out for wines from La Livinière, a sub-region in Minervois. Otherwise, look for Côteaux du Languedoc on the front label. These wines are great with slow-cooked stews, especially coq au vin or beef, lamb or just a simple mushroom risotto.

SPANISH REDS FROM OFF-THE-BEATEN-TRACK REGIONS

Yes, there's Rioja. And I love a good Rioja. But go off the beaten track, east in fact, to a region called Yecla. Here, the wines are made from a red grape called Monastrell. Bright, juicy and capable of warming even the coldest cockles. Or there's the region of Bierzo, in north-west Spain, where the Mencia grape produces wines with real personality (intense, dark, fruit-laden little beasties). These wines are brilliant with a spicy chorizo and chicken Spanish stew or a simple tomato-based pasta dish with a bit of spice.

CHILEAN REDS FROM THE MAULE REGION

You'll find all the big hitters in this region in Chile's Central Valley: Cabernet Sauvignon, Merlot, Shiraz, Pinot Noir. But there's also other stuff to try, including Carignan and Cabernet Franc. Underrated and so often good value, these wines are rich, smooth and, above all, warming. Put a Chilean Cabernet with chilli, Shiraz with steak and Pinot Noir with stuffed peppers.

AUSTRALIAN REDS FROM THE YARRA VALLEY REGION

This is a cool-climate region in Victoria, Australia, and one that has a reputation for producing tear-inducing Pinot Noir wines. Not because of the price, as many red Burgundies do, but because of their standout quality. They are lighter in style than Pinot from other regions in Australia, and more perfumed, but that makes them versatile, especially when it comes to food. Try Yarra Pinot with scallops and bacon: definitely worth a go.

ARGENTINIAN REDS FROM THE MENDOZA REGION

Look for cooler-climate names on the front label, including Luján de Cuyo, where there are Malbecs, Cabernet Sauvignons and even great Tempranillo wines to choose from. By law, you have to put these with a steak. Chips too, of course.

So there you go. Your fireside homework. We'll do the same for whites and rosé in a bit. But for now, grab a glass of fireside red, a cashmere blanket and sit by the fire. Or, in my case, a rug that smells faintly of cat pee and a broken gas fire (nice). But as long as the children are in bed, the Husband is home and the wine is good, I'm happy. Not SAD. Next, we're talking store cupboards and Dirty Prosecco. Obviously.

TRUE OR FALSE: SCREW CAPS ARE ONLY FOR CHEAP WINES

Not any more. Screw caps have been around for a long time and were originally associated with cheap and not-so-cheerful wines. A handful of pioneering winemakers from the New World, noticeably New Zealand, started using them back in the 1970s for their smarter wines as an alternative to traditional corks. The reason they wanted an alternative to cork was a chemical compound known as TCA, which is the cause of wines being 'corked'.

If a wine is described as corked, it doesn't mean there are bits of cork floating in it (if that happens, blame it on the corkscrew, or a poor quality or very old cork). What it means is that the wine smells odd, which can range from slightly dusty-odd to really horrid damp dishcloth-odd. However badly it is affected, the wine is not nice to drink. It's caused by a reaction between the wine and the TCA, which sits in the natural cork, and there is no way of knowing if a bottle is affected until it's opened. At the height of the problem, before screw-capped wines became mainstream, the rate of cork taint was around one in every twelve bottles.

Things are very different now, with screw caps being used on all quality levels. As one winemaker put it, using a screw cap meant that their wine would reach the drinker just as they intended: fresh and cork-taint free. There are some who still screw their noses at the screw cap, but the majority of wines are still sealed with a natural cork and there seems to be room for both. I'm just relieved we're not using camel dung wrapped in muslin, which is what we did before the Romans started using cork. Progress is impossible without change, as they say.

CHAPTER
FIVE

STORE-CUPBOARD SOS

In a perfect world, my fridge and kitchen cupboards would look like the inside cover of one of Nigella's cookery books. I can't remember which particular book it was, but it gave me store-cupboard envy. In reality, we have definite peaks and troughs in this house when it comes to stocking the store cupboard. Sometimes I am on it like a bonnet and get my online order done and booked, ready for delivery at the start of the week. However, it is more likely to be me plus one, two or – if I'm really disorganized – three very bored and tired children trawling the aisles after school. What I do know is this: as long as we have dried pasta, a tin of tuna and a can of sweetcorn in the house, we can survive anything. I know, no fresh vegetables, but we're talking store-cupboard essentials.

Just as we have food-store-cupboard essentials, so I have wine ones. Obviously. These are the wines that, over the years, I have learnt to always keep a bottle of in stock, at all times. They just make life taste better, as it were. And what elevates them from normal drinks to store-cupboard drinks is their all-year-round suitability for drinking and cooking. So useful! The oomph in a red-wine stew? That'll be the wine. The zing with pan-fried scallops, covered in just the tiniest bit of juice deglazed from the pan at the last minute? Wine, again.

COOKING WITH WINE

I was once told that you shouldn't cook with wine that you wouldn't drink. That doesn't really narrow it down for me. Sure, don't cook with wine that has something wrong with it, for example a wine that is corked (see page 76 for an explanation of what corked wine is). But when it comes to using wine in cooking, what I use depends on how much I need. I'm not going to waste a good bottle of wine by tipping half of it into the cooking pot, thank you very much. No, if the recipe calls for a generous quantity of wine (Jamie's stews and Nigella's casseroles are the usual suspects here), then I go for a simple red or white from the bottom shelf; the cheapest I can find from France or Spain normally deliver the goods. You want sound, quality wine that won't make you wince as you pour it into a pot.

If the recipe calls for a splash of wine (Nigel Slater is one for adding a dash, wonderfully frugal as he is), then I use whatever I have open. On Sundays, the wine used in the gravy is taken from whatever wine we have open on the table to drink, regardless of colour. Don't be tempted to keep a wine on the side for weeks to use in cooking when you need it, as wine doesn't stay fresh in the bottle for more than a few days after opening. Once air is in contact with the wine, the process of oxidation begins, changing the wine's character so that it loses its fruit. Leave it for longer than a few days and it will change colour (lighter for reds, darker for whites), and after a week or so it will be completely knackered. Using a wine that has been open for a while (or which has had air in the bottle), so that it has that oxidized, perhaps even vinegar character, won't do your food any favours.

Bag-in-box wines, however, keep fresh for much longer, up to four weeks in most cases. Many a restaurant will have bag-in-box wine on hand for this purpose, you just don't see it (more on bag-in-box wine later).

Let's look at good store-cupboard wines for cooking.

✱ WHITE WINE

If the recipe calls for more than a dash of white wine, then you want to use something with flavours that won't clash with or overpower the food. This is where the pleasant but fairly neutral flavours of a South African or Australian white (usually made from a blend of grapes) or a cheap Italian

Pinot Grigio are useful: sometimes a bit boring to drink but perfect for cooking. If you use a strongly flavoured wine, like a really oaky Chardonnay, the end result will be a bit weird. It's the same as using a very aromatic grape such as Gewürztraminer (more on that later). Unless the dish calls specifically for a type of wine, go for the simple white-blend option.

✳ RED WINE

Here, we're into hearty stew territory, when the recipe says, 'Pour in 300ml of red wine.' That's roughly half a bottle. As mentioned, I'm not going to pour really lovely wine into a cooking pot, but I'm happy to pour wine I wouldn't *mind* drinking into it. So, if I'm doing a party-piece lamb stew for friends, I'll use a basic Côtes du Rhône, if it's not too expensive. If the wine's going into something with a bit of spice, then I'll go cheaper and pick a basic French red. I know that beef bourguignon should be made with a red Burgundy, but seriously, I can't bring myself to pour wine that costs that much into a pot. I'd rather pour it slowly down my neck.

✳ ROSÉ WINE

I've noticed more recipes calling for a splash or glug of rosé to be added. Again, don't use anything smart, but avoid anything sweet too, because this will affect the flavour of the dish. Stay away from the Californian Blush wines, unless you want your cooking to taste a bit sweet. Dry Spanish rosé wines are great value and fit the bill perfectly, as you can add some to the pot and stick the rest in the fridge to drink later.

✳ VERMOUTH

This is a brilliant cooking ingredient, bringing even the most basic risotto to life and adding bite to a dish. Noilly Prat is my favourite, a dry white vermouth made from the Picpoul and Clairette grapes from the area around Marseille in southern France, not that you can tell, because by the time it's made it tastes of all sorts of things, namely chamomile and lemons. It has an almost medicinal quality – and I mean that in a good way. This particular vermouth is made by ageing wine outside in huge oak casks throughout all four seasons, and its taste comes from the addition of a secret concoction of twenty botanicals, including orange peel and nutmeg. In hot weather, a small glass of this over lots of ice makes a gorgeous aperitif. It's a store-cupboard essential if ever there was one and it will keep in the fridge for a good few months once opened.

✳ MARSALA

This fortified wine – meaning a wine with spirit added to it – is from Sicily in Italy and adds a wonderful dark richness to a dish. Usually made from the Grillo, Inzolia or Catarratto grapes, the Italians use Marsala in lots of dishes, but it seems to have a natural fondness for chicken, mushrooms and beef (not all at the same time), especially when slugged into a pan sticky with meat sauces and mixed with a bit of cream. Marsala varies in sweetness depending on style, but they can all be used for cooking. We're talking dashes and slugs rather than big quantities, as the flavour of Marsala is pretty out there. I keep mine in the cupboard rather than the fridge (I've already got Noilly Prat in the fridge, plus wine, so I don't have room for the Marsala too. Unless I get a separate drinks fridge. Now there's an idea . . .). I'm sure it tastes better within the first few months, but ours lasts for the best part of a year. Proper store-cupboard stuff.

✳ THINKING OUTSIDE THE BOX

Speaking of which, we need to talk about bag-in-box wines. They used to get a very bad rap almost everywhere, being considered the vinous equivalent of a pot noodle. In Australia, where the form originated, namely a wine bag inside a box, they are called cask wines. This makes them sound inexpensive, but not horrible. The name we use, bag-in-box, manages to make it sound both cheap and horrible, which is a shame because nowadays many of the bag-in-box wines found on our shelves are not bad. In fact, some are positively brilliant.

Nowadays it's not just thin French reds and tasteless

Liebfraumilch clogging up the bottom shelves. Instead, if you know what to look for you will find wines with lots of flavour and personality, not just boring cheap stuff. New Zealand Sauvignon Blanc, Côtes du Rhône and and Provence rosé, to name but a few, can all be found in bag-in-box form, and because the packaging is cheaper to produce than glass bottles, the wine inside is usually pretty good value.

If you need more reasons to give bag-in-box wines a try, how about a) the wine keeps fresh for longer as there's no air in the bag, so you can keep one in your fridge for up to four weeks and b) they do less damage to the environment than glass bottles (glass is energy-hungry to produce and heavy to transport). Sadly, however, bag-in-box packaging has become synonymous with cheap and nasty wines – just as we used to think of screw-capped wines. Perhaps it's time to think outside the box?

As a rule of thumb, go for ones with a simple, modern label and go one step up from the cheapest. Australia, Chile and France are good, reliable sources of inexpensive, versatile wines made to please a crowd. Keep one each of red and white in the store cupboard, just behind the pasta, tuna and tinned sweetcorn.

✳ SHERRY

Sherry is one of the most misunderstood wines of all. It can be light and bone dry, or syrup-thick and sweet. The cheap sweet stuff has given the rest a bad name, which is a great shame because the good stuff can be divine and amazing value for money. When it comes to cooking, sherry is an inspired ingredient for soups, stews and, of course, puddings (my mum's Christmas sherry trifle should be on prescription). But before we decide what to cook with, let's look at what there is to drink, as this is far more important.

What is Sherry?

Sherry is made mainly from the light-skinned Palomino grape in Spain's most southern – and very hot – province, Andalucia. To be called sherry, it must come from the sherry triangle, marked by the towns of Jerez de la Frontera (from which sherry takes it name; we Brits just couldn't pronounce Jerez) and the coastal towns of Sanlúcar de Barrameda and El Puerto de Santa María. The best vineyards are on chalky albariza soils.

What Does it Taste Like?

Sherry ranges from bone dry to candy sweet, depending on style. The two basic dry styles are Fino and Manzanilla, both of which are very pale in colour and positively quivering with nervous tension. They taste tangy (due to *flor* – more on that in a mo). Then there are dry amber-coloured Amontillado and darker Oloroso styles, both nutty in flavour and, in the case of Oloroso, aged for much longer in oak barrels. If you want *good* sweet, there's the dark treacle-like PX, made from the Pedro Ximénez grapes.

Flor! What is it Good For?

Flor is a strange yeast beast, unique to the Jerez region, and it grows as a delicate film on top of the wine in the barrel, protecting it from air (and oxidation). *Flor* needs around 15.5 per cent alcohol to thrive, so base wines are fortified with spirit to reach at least that, sometimes more depending on what style of sherry is being made. Wines aged in bodegas (cellars) in the more humid coastal town of Sanlúcar are called Manzanilla and possess seaside saltiness (although I do wonder if this is partly due to the salted almonds I shovel in when sipping it). *Flor* doesn't survive on the higher-alcohol Amontillado or Oloroso styles, so the wines oxidize and darken in colour as they age in oak, developing stronger flavours.

Should it be Aged?

Actually, by the time you buy it, it's pretty much good to go. It's aged as it's made, via a solera system. Barrels known as sherry butts are stacked up on top of each other in a pyramid in the bodegas and a proportion of older wines are taken out at this blending stage and replaced with younger wines. The older and more layered the solera system, the subtler the resulting wine should be. Over the years producers have developed their own consistent styles, similar but unique. Drink Fino and Manzanilla within days of opening the bottle. Darker styles will last a bit longer.

So What Else Makes Sherry Interesting?
Complex and interesting, it's the mix of young and often very old wine and the exhausting range of styles that makes it interesting. Dry Fino and Manzanilla is best served really cold in small measures as a pre-prandial (tapas-style nibbles essential). Amontillado and Oloroso (meaning 'scented') is best served when curled up in front of a fire. PX is almost always poured over ice cream in this house (adults only, obv).

What Should I Buy?
Sherry can make for complicated shopping. Luckily, there are some very trusty producers to look out for. Some of them make wines for supermarket own labels too, making them brilliant value. Here's a shortlist: Lustau, Hidalgo, Gonzales Byass, Valdespino, Osborne.

COOKS' PERKS

So we've got store-cupboard wines for cooking sorted, but what about the cook? I'm talking about the small glass you have before food, the palate pick-me-up enjoyed in the kitchen. A glass of very chilled Fino or Manzanilla sherry does that job very well, as does a small Noilly Prat. And then there's Campari. I adore Campari, a jewel-coloured weird blend of fruit, herbs, water and alcohol. I love the classic, no-nonsense bottle, the brilliant label and the fact that it is the essential ingredient for both a Dirty Prosecco (just add a dash of Campari to a glass of Prosecco) and an Americano (one part Campari, one part red vermouth, topped up with as much soda as you like). Swap the soda for gin and you transform the Americano into a Negroni, the ultimate mother's little helper.

Another store-cupboard essential, at least in this house, is Amaretto. I know, it's sweet, dark, tastes of almonds and is slightly sickly. I've tipped it into syllabubs and used it in cream sauces to accompany pork chops, but I love it best served with huge chunks of ice at the end of a celebratory dinner, usually at Christmas.

So, your store-cupboard essentials should look like this:

* 1 half-bottle of Fino or Manzanilla sherry
* 1 bottle of Marsala
* 1 bottle of Noilly Prat
* 1 bottle of Campari
* 1 bottle of Amaretto (optional)
* 1 bag-in-box of inexpensive dry white wine (Australian or South African)
* 1 bag-in-box of inexpensive red wine (French or Australian)

WHAT IS THE DIFFERENCE BETWEEN TASTE AND FLAVOUR?

Taste is all about characteristics in food, wine, whatever, which we can measure using our palates (our tongue). We can taste four distinct sensations: bitterness, sweetness, saltiness and acidity. Then there's umami, now widely recognized as the fifth taste, and best described as savouriness or even deliciousness. Umami is a Japanese word and is found in foods like mushrooms, soy sauce, oily fish and ripe fruits. Oysters are rich in umami. As is breast milk, apparently. Not that I'm suggesting you try it that way. Better to buy a tube of umami – available in all good middle-class stores – and add it to broths. Either that or ship in the oysters.

The difference between taste and flavour is that the latter involves smell. It's a more complex, personal sensation than taste and allows taste and smell to work together to create a unique flavour sensation. This helps to explain why some people are more sensitive to certain flavours than others, because the way our sense of smell and taste interact is unique to each one of us. In fact, unless you are an identical twin, you are the only person in the world to smell like you do. I don't mean how you *smell*, I mean how *you* smell. I know you know what I mean. All this talk of food is making me hungry.

Dinner time, I think.

CHAPTER

SIX

DINNER TIME –
TV, KITCHEN OR POSH

Dear Masterchef,

I thought I could do it. I thought I could go cold turkey, perhaps even use the time I used to spend with you doing something more productive. I could take up the hem on the trousers I bought over a month ago, maybe finish the book I've been reading for the last two.

Of course, I'd forgotten how seductive you are, with your cooking-with-medical-urgency theme tune, your big-swell music when you announce the finalists, your increasingly tenuous celebrity contestants (who I usually love by the end) and your shouty presenters that cry when they hit on a culinary revelation. Even though I thought you needed a format makeover – perhaps that's why I thought I could walk away – I now realize you are like a pair of favourite slippers: worn but perfectly comfortable. So here we are again, older, wiser and wondering how on earth certain celebs get through life without knowing what's in an omelette. Thank you, for everything.

Love, Knackered Mother

Now, I do really love cooking. Or at least I did until I became rather too familiar with the kitchen, churning out food for people big and small at all times of the day. Oh, the hours spent puréeing random fruit and veg combinations only to have them met with tiny, pursed rosebud lips belonging to various babies (I'm looking at you, Annabel Karmel). Add those to the time spent blowtorching dried cereal from the table and mopping up spilt drinks and you can see why 'cooking' lost its shine.

During those dark days I found joy through watching other people cook lovely stuff on TV, which they could do without having to shop, peel veg or small children from their legs, or even wash up. However, the kitchen fog lifted once we were done with puréed food and I slowly fell back in love with cooking. We still have our moments, but mostly we're good.

What I never stopped loving, obviously, was wine. I hold the theory that even the most lax of meals – beans on toast, jackets with cheese, cheese and crackers – can be transformed by a simple glass of wine. Obviously I am not talking children's tea any more, unless you've had a really bad day. But there's dinner, and then there's *dinner*, and what you drink with it is determined by the occasion and what you are eating. This is when it gets interesting. Are we talking dinner on your lap in front of the TV? Or perhaps you plan to put on some lippy and go all 'date night'? Is it dinner for one, or dinner for ten? Is the boss coming for dinner? Whatever the occasion – slob, kitchen or posh – we need to look at the part-art, part-science deal of matching food and wine in more detail.

MATCHING FOOD AND WINE: THE BASICS

There are lots of unofficial 'rules' when it comes to matching food with wine, the most obvious one being red wine with meat, white wine with fish. I happen to think that's not strictly true. If you are going to remember just one rule about matching food and wine, make it this one: *Think about the weight of flavour of the food you are about to scoff and try and match it with a wine of a similar weight.* Here, weight refers to the body and fullness of the wine. This, of course, means there are endless possible combinations and some will work better than others. However, I like the trial and error aspect of it all. Apart from when I get it horribly wrong. Which, although annoying, isn't really the end of the world. It is, however, a waste and I do so hate waste. There is also the question of whether a wine needs food at all. I say yes it does, to make it taste better and to avoid getting a hangover. So, you've got your one simple rule memorized – match weight of dish to the weight of wine – and here's how you do that.

First of all, think about how the dish in question is cooked, and what it's cooked with. The wine needs to be able to cope with the dominant flavour of the dish. How it is cooked – steamed, grilled, fried or roasted, or even raw in a salad – calls for wines of different weight. Know this and you have a better chance of matching your dish with a wine that will complement rather than dominate the food. You want to be able to taste both food and wine, not just one or the other. Before we look at actual ingredients, we need to understand what it is about wine that affects tastes. (If any of these words look unfamiliar, check back to chapter two).

* **Acidity:** in wine, acidity helps to cut through oily, creamy or salty food. Oily fish needs wine with 'bite'.
* **Sweetness:** natural sweetness in a wine is fantastic when it matches sweetness in a dish. We're talking puddings, especially.
* **Body:** the golden rule is to match the body – the weight – of the wine to the weight of the dish. A big beef stew will suffocate a delicate, light white wine, while a spicy Côtes du Rhône will shout down a beautifully delicate fish dish.
* **Oak:** in wine, oak adds weight and complexity, so it calls for a dish with oomph. That beef stew will do nicely.
* **Tannin:** here's another science bit. The tannins in red wine (see page 15 for a reminder) help to break down the protein and fat in (mostly red) meats. Like Fred and Ginger, red wine and red meats were made for each other.

Let's put these basics into practice and have a look at specific ingredients.

✳ FISH

Generally speaking, a dry white wine will suit fish more than a red wine will. Chablis, with its steely acidity and (usual) lack of oak makes it a timeless classic for many a simple white fish dish. However, if the fish has got a stronger flavour, such as salmon or tuna, then you can branch into red wine territory. Not a great big tannic beast, but something with soft tannins, Pinot Noir for example, can work brilliantly. For oily fish such as smoked salmon, something with lots of acidity and 'bite' to help cut through the oiliness is the way to go. It's a cliché, but smoked salmon and Champagne is a knockout combination. For sushi lovers, wine with a bit of natural sweetness works a treat; look for something with 'late harvest' on the label. If grilled prawns are on the menu, you have to drink it with Manzanilla (which you now have in your fridge, thanks to your store-cupboard essentials list).

✳ CHICKEN AND OTHER BIRDS

As you now know, it's as much about the way the chicken is cooked and what it's served with as it is to do with the actual meat. Simple roast chicken with salad loves a creamy, fruity Chardonnay, with a bit of oak perhaps, but add all the trimmings of a big Sunday roast and you'll find that a smooth medium-bodied red does the trick. If you're a game bird, go for Pinot Noir.

✳ RED MEAT

The fuller flavours of red meat demand fuller flavours from the wine it's going to be eaten with, but there are some things to watch out for. Tannin can clash with fat, so if you've got a fatty piece of meat, avoid very tannic reds. Go for Cabernet Sauvignon over Cabernet Franc, for example. Again, think about the weight of the flavours from the meat – and whatever sauce you've got with it – and try to balance it with a red that will stand up to it but not shout over it.

✳ VEGETABLES

Annoyingly, veggie dishes do present some fairly random challenges when it comes to matching them with the right sort of wines. Tomatoes are relatively high in acidity, so match them with a wine that has the same, such as cooler-climate white wines; Sauvignon Blanc is especially good. Another one is asparagus, which can make some white wines taste almost like tin. Not that I've eaten tin, but hopefully you'll know what I'm driving at, a sort of metallic taste. I rather like Riesling with asparagus, as it happens. Simple salads call for simple white wines: Pinot Grigio works well. An omelette just needs a glass of crisp, dry white wine, such as unoaked Chardonnay (Chablis, for example) or Gavi (an Italian white made from the Cortese grape) or

Pinot Gris from Alsace or New Zealand. And then there's rosé: highly underrated in the veggie food matching stakes. Believe me, there are endless great combinations.

✳ HERBY FOOD

If you're faced with a plate of food that's absolutely covered in a particular herb, and that herb is going to be the dominant flavour in the dish, you need to find a wine that likes it. Pick a rosé to accompany thyme. Go for a dry Muscat if you're minted (herb-wise, not cash-wise). Basil loves Italian whites, while rosemary prefers a red, especially if served with lamb.

✳ SPICY FOOD

This is a tricky one as there are so many varying degrees of spiciness in foods. The really spicy stuff – hotter-than-hot curries for example – leave the taste buds wanting something cool and refreshing with a fairly neutral flavour. Beer will cleanse the palate, but it won't really work with the food. Rather, it turns its back on it. If, however, the food isn't so spicy as to render your taste buds helpless, then wine can have a look in.

Asian-influenced food is very happy with a dry or off-dry white wine, especially fruity ones with a good lick of acidity. Gewürztraminer is a case in point, and the literal meaning of *gewürz* is spice. Made for each other, clearly. Stay away from oaky wines; they don't get along so well with spice

– call it an awkward relationship. Spicy red meat dishes are better off with a fruity Australian Shiraz, whilst a drier, more tannic or oaky red is more likely to clash with the spice in the dish.

✳ PUDDINGS

I have seen people get really excited about matching chocolate with red wine. There are courses, books and blogs dedicated to it. I have tried it, extensively. Once upon a time, in my role as a wine buyer, I was asked to find out what wine went best with chocolate. I was put in a room with about forty types of chocolate (bars, puddings, you name it) and about a hundred different wines of all styles and colours. I was then told not to come out until I'd found perfect matches. I promise you, I am not making this up. A team of us tasted, sniffed, sipped and spat (ew, sorry) our way round that tasting table. And the verdict? Mostly, wine and chocolate is a tricky match. Wine's acidity and/or tannins fight with the sweetness of chocolate. But every now and again, a particular combination works brilliantly. It really is a case of trial and error.

At the end of a long dinner I am usually the one with the box of After Eights in front of me, building up a little pile of empty paper envelopes, the contents of which have been popped in my mouth with a little shudder of consciousness as each one goes in. Red wine doesn't usually work *that* well with chocolate, unless it is a big, rich, almost chocolatey New World red (try a smart Australian Shiraz or South African Pinotage), but by that stage my taste buds are a little overwhelmed, so they don't argue.

If you are going to match a wine with pudding, then do it with style. A sweet wine is a better match for chocolate, Banyuls or Maury from France particularly. These are fortified sweet wines from the South of France and they crop up again a bit later on. If you've got a fruit-based pudding, Prosecco is a revelation because it has that sweetness and froth to make it both balance the flavours of the dish and refresh it at the same time. I realize that I now have three different types of wine on the table, but mixing your wine styles will not give you a hangover (if drunk in moderation).

✳ CHEESE

Lots of different types of cheese work best with different styles of wine, but again, a few guidelines are blue with sweet (think Stilton and Sauternes or port) and hard-flavoured cheese with bigger reds (the big-hitting Italian Amarone is one to try). Soft cheese likes aromatic whites. Again, one of nature's party tricks is to create a cheese somewhere and then ensure the local wine is an almost unbeatable match. If you haven't tried the goats' cheese from Chavignol with a white wine from Sancerre, can I suggest you do? Add it to your bucket list. Sometimes I go for just one type of strong cheese – albeit a fairly big hunk – and have a bottle of fruity red in the wings. No one's complained yet.

WHAT WINE WHEN?

Life is too short for lots of things. Stuffing a mushroom, for one (Shirley Conran). Too short to be livin' with stress, for another (Dizzee Rascal). Whilst I agree with both Shirley and Dizzee, my own personal favourite, unsurprisingly, is that life's too short to drink bad wine. Obviously, you should drink whatever you are in the mood for, it's just that by putting a bit of thought into the matching bit, you can improve a meal no end. And if you are cooking something that requires some effort and time, why not bring out the best in the flavours with a wine that supports the dish rather than works against it? By opening the right bottle mid-week, you can perk up even the slackest meal by making the flavours sing rather than mumble. And by putting the right bottles on the table when someone important comes for dinner, you can look ever so knowledgeable (which, having read all this, you now are).

The thing is, you need to put it into practice in order to learn from experience. Here are some combinations to try, both classic and not so classic. Remember to scribble a note in your posh notebook/on your phone so that you can repeat the successful pairings and avoid the ones you don't like. Not that any of these ones won't work; believe me, I've done my homework.

Dish – main ingredients	Classic pairing	Not-so-classic pairing
Simple salad	Pinot Grigio	Picpoul de Pinet (southern French white)
Mushroom risotto	Chianti	Chilean Pinot Noir
Thai fish curry	Gewürztraminer from Alsace	Australian Pinot Gris
Burger	Cabernet Sauvignon from anywhere	Californian Zinfandel
Five-spice pork belly	New Zealand Pinot Noir	New Zealand Chardonnay
Lamb chops with herb butter	Red Bordeaux (Cabernet/Merlot blend)	Argentinian Malbec
Chicken curry (mild)	Beer	Champagne (not kidding)
Lasagne	Chianti	Southern Italian Red (Primitivo, Nero d'Avola)

And here, I give you slack snack matches, best enjoyed in front of the TV, conversation optional:

✳ BEANS ON TOAST

Add a dash of HP sauce and match it with a New World Shiraz or Malbec. If you don't like HP, stick with a soft, juicy Spanish red made from the Tempranillo grape or a red from the South of France with the Carignan grape in it.

✳ CHEESE AND CRACKERS

This is my Sunday night staple; call it a ritual even. After a fairly hefty Sunday roast, I still have to have something to eat in the evening to mark it and put off the Sunday night blues. The Husband usually makes it for me (he has a full fry-up – not joking) and it's eaten on the sofa with a glass of whatever we've got left over from lunch, as long as it's red. In a perfect world this would be a glass of Amarone (an Italian red) with hard cheese, but a splash of Rioja is just as heart-warming.

✳ BOWL OF CEREAL

You are clearly too tired for food. Or wine, for that matter. You need hot chocolate in your state.

TRUE OR FALSE? GOOD WINE SHOULD BE DECANTED

The point of decanting wine is to separate the wine from any sediment that may be floating about in the bottle, particularly wines with a lot of sediment, such as port. The best way to do this is stand the bottle upright for a few hours before drinking and then slowly, but in one go, pour the wine into a decanter, leaving the sediment in the bottle. Another reason to decant is to let it 'breathe' – let air get to the wine for a short while before drinking.

Whether you need to do it or not depends on the wine, the occasion and the time you have. In general, when we've got friends/in-laws over and we're opening a really good bottle, I do one of two things. If feeling grand, I pour it into the one and only decanter we have (a wedding present with the obligatory chip on the neck) about an hour beforehand and leave it on the table. If not feeling that grand, or just not organized enough, I simply decant the bottle into a glass jug, then pour it back into the bottle and plonk it on the table. This simple act means that the wine has been aerated – albeit quickly.

If you think about it, once poured the wine will sit in the glass for a while anyway (we're talking big glasses, obviously). A rich, complex red or a layered, textured white will open up and develop in the glass over time. Having said that, if left exposed to the air for too long the wine will lose its impact, much as a perfume wears off after a time. Very old wines will dissipate at a quicker rate as the structure of the wine is so delicate. Just keep sipping and enjoy how it changes over time.

Next up, it's Christmas time. There's no need to be afraid. After the next chapter, you'll be festive match-fit.

CHAPTER

SEVEN

THE BIG ONES –
CHRISTMAS AND NEW YEAR

Ah, Christmas. A time for giving and receiving, but no time for having a little lie down in a darkened room, which is what us knackered mothers really need. First, there's the end-of-term school marathon of nativity plays, carol concerts, class bauble-decorating competitions and a seemingly endless call for mince pies. Then there is the Christmas Plan, deciding where you are going to be, and when, on the big day. Living in the same village as my parents and in-laws, we are lucky enough not to have to spend the festive period in the car moving around the country. Rather, we've had years of moving like a little pack of Vicar of Dibleys from one end of the village to the other, eating and drinking as we go. Even so, this requires some level of diplomacy and a certain pacing of one's consumption. Then, a few years ago, we thought we'd do Christmas dinner at ours, and it has been so ever since.

As much as I tell myself that cooking on Christmas Day is no more than cooking a very large roast, we all know it's not that simple. For a start, there is the weight of expectation. Weeks of being bombarded with TV adverts that make you weep (thanks, John Lewis), Sunday supplements stuffed with food porn designed to make you feel inadequate, and present-buying that always, *always* has me praying at the altar of Amazon late at night. I can't believe how ridiculous we are about presents nowadays. When I was little, I used to get a stocking with a tape cassette (Abba's *Super Trouper* was possibly one of the best things I was ever given), a party popper, a walnut and a satsuma. That was it. The Husband grew up with a pillowcase. Seriously, he and his three siblings got a *pillowcase* stuffed full with presents. So when we had our first Christmas as parents, we had the stocking/pillowcase talk: what to do for our own children? Of course, the pillowcase won.

Anyway, back to the very large roast. I take up any offers of help; this is no time to be a martyr. My mother and mother-in-law both come armed with trimmings (here, natural competitiveness works very much in my favour. I am yet to make my own cranberry sauce, but I am sure my time will come). And I am always in charge of drinks. With all the time and effort spent on the feast, the same attention should be afforded to the drinks, given that they can make or break a meal. I know this all sounds terribly dramatic but please indulge me. Honestly, the wrong wine can sit all over the food or even slip down unnoticed. I know the latter is sometimes what's called for, but not here, not now. So, here's how to do Christmas Day wine with ease, or at least less shouting.

CHRISTMAS MORNING - A SPLASH OF SOMETHING FIZZY

This is my Christmas treat: a small glass of something fizzy in the kitchen whilst getting things ready, quite possibly in my dressing gown. Others can help themselves too – they usually do. A good Prosecco has a gentle fizz, a touch of sweetness and a definite festive feel. Try and find one from the Valdobbiadene region, a small area in Italy, near Venice, recognized for making fizz from the Glera grape that is a quality notch above the rest. In recent years, the growing selection of Crémant on the shelves has given us good reason to crack open something that tastes a lot like Champagne but at (usually) half the price. If you don't finish it, pop it back in the fridge with a wine stopper lightly placed on the top and save it to drink as a palate-cleanser later on.

CHRISTMAS LUNCH OR DINNER

Because of all the different flavours that go on the table food-wise, have both a white and red wine lined up. I usually wait until the last few weeks before Christmas to buy the wine, otherwise I might miss a good deal or we'll drink it all before the big day. The shelves are awash with wine deals at Christmas, but you need to navigate your way through them with care. Some aren't quite as good as they look. If buying in quantity, always try a bottle first to save making an expensive mistake.

MULLING IT OVER

No Christmas would be complete without mulled wine. Most supermarkets now sell pre-spiced mulled wine in bottles, so all you have to do is pour it into the pan and warm it up, but I do think it is worth the effort of starting with a base red and making a special 'house recipe' with your own measures of cinnamon, cloves, ginger, honey, oranges and lemons. (Don't you feel Christmassy already?)

Go for a robust red so that it has at least half a chance of matching up to the earthy spices: southern French or Chilean reds are great value for mulling and you can add a splash of port for extra va-va-voom. As you stir and taste, think about the balance of flavours. Too sweet? Add more spice. Too spicy? Add more wine and sugar. Whatever you do, don't overheat the wine – this will give it a horrible metallic taste, and you'll burn off all the alcohol. A very bad idea, obviously.

Here's a trusted recipe: Pour 100ml of orange juice into a pan. Heat slowly, adding 100g of muscovado sugar. Once combined, add half an orange, studded with 5 cloves. Next, add a sliced vanilla pod, a peeled thumb of fresh ginger, one stick of cinnamon, a piece of dried star anise and a bottle of red wine (or roughly the same amount, i.e. 75cl, from your bag-in-box you've got in the store cupboard). Then add 50ml of ruby port and let it all sit together in the pan on a gentle heat for about 10 minutes (no boiling, remember). When you are ready to go, sieve the liquid into a jug, pour and imbibe. Heartily.

✳ SMOKED SALMON

As I have explained, oily fish needs a white wine with good acidity to cut through and balance it. Sometimes, only Champagne will do, and Christmas Day is one of those times. You are better off going for a good, trusty own-label Brut Non-Vintage (NV) Champagne or a favourite well-known brand than a never-seen-before half-price deal. Take it from me; I've done the research. Trade secret: the Tesco Finest Premier Cru Champagne is the one that beat most big-name Champagne brands in a blind tasting carried out by *Which?* magazine years ago, and it is still sourced from the same producers. I used to be responsible for buying it when I was a wine buyer there, so I come back and taste it as often as I can find a good reason to, just to check how it's doing. Happy to report it's still unbelievably good value at under £20. Don't go telling everyone, they might put the price up.

✳ TURKEY (AND OTHER BIRDS)

On its own, turkey is easy to match with a wine because, well, it isn't the most exciting flavour in the world. You could put it with red, white, rosé or a sparkling wine and it would be quite happy. But, it's Christmas, and the plate is piled with other stuff that isn't so easy to match. Cranberry sauce is a fairly dominant flavour, as are sprouts, and sausages wrapped in bacon. Chablis – which is made from the Chardonnay grape – is often touted as the fail-safe match for turkey, and so it is, but I prefer a rounder, almost creamier Chardonnay to cope with the mixed bag of savoury flavours on the plate at Christmas. A dry white with a bit more body (see page 39), such as Chardonnay or Viognier with a touch of oak from France, a Chenin Blanc from South Africa, or an Australian Semillon, all match up well with the food. Being naturally greedy sorts, we have red on the table too, to take us from turkey to cheese.

The classic red pairing for turkey is Pinot Noir, especially red Burgundy from France. If you want classic, Rully is a name to look out for (it's often pretty good value for money too, being a lesser-known appellation than its more famous near-neighbours). But as lovely as classic is, in recent years I've gone for something gutsier with great results. A Rhône red such as a Crozes-Hermitage or Châteauneuf-du-Pape is appropriately glitzy, as are the usually slightly better value but lesser-known wines from nearby Vacqueyras or Gigondas, all made from a combination cocktail of southern Rhône grape varieties, including Grenache, Syrah, Mourvèdre and Cinsault (among others). You're looking at spending around £15–20 a bottle.

If goose is going on the table, there's a bit more flavour, which calls for wine with acidity to cut through the fattier meat. Enter stage left, Italian reds. They work wonders, especially anything made from the Nebbiolo grape, with its trademark high acidity (Barolo, for example), or a Chianti Classico, made primarily from the Sangiovese grape.

✳ RED MEATS

As you now know, red meats work well with red wines as the tannins in the wine help break down the protein in the meat, so 'softening' the tannins. An Argentinian Malbec on the table will bring out the juicy flavours in both the meat and wine, as will a jolly good Claret (red Bordeaux, usually a blend of Cabernet Sauvignon and Merlot).

If you are hamming it up, the flavour of ham is better matched with a red, but the saltiness of the meat requires something not too tannic (they can be uncomfortable bedfellows). Here, Gamay is great but Pinot Noir really is the answer, especially from France, but also from Chile, New Zealand or Australia. If the recipe means the ham has a fair bit of sweetness, in the glaze for example, then match it with a bit of natural fruit sweetness in the wine. A Chilean Cabernet Sauvignon from the Colchagua Valley is a tried-and-tested favourite with a cola-covered ham joint (Google the recipe!).

✳ CHEESE

Port is the traditional drink to hit the table when the cheese comes out and there is something undeniably Christmassy about passing the port. Etiquette (and there is a lot of port etiquette) dictates that the decanter keeps moving around the table to the left until it is finished, and if someone holds on to it longer than they should, one asks, 'Do you know the Bishop of Norwich?' so prompting the port hogger in question to pass it on. However, I find that yelling, 'Oi! Pass the bloody port, will you?' works just as well. Here's a quick guide to port styles, which should help you through:

Port – What is it All About?

Port is a fortified wine, meaning that grape spirit is added to the wine, thus making it stronger and, well, 'fortifying' it. In the case of port, it is added before fermentation is complete, stopping the wine from fermenting further (unlike sherry, when it is added after fermentation). The result is fairly alcoholic wine with a natural sweetness (as not all the sugar is fermented).

The wine is made from grapes grown in the Douro Valley in Portugal, and whilst there are a huge number of different grape varieties allowed, the blends are usually made up from around twenty different varieties, including Touriga Nacional, Touriga Franca and Tinta Roriz. And one called Bastardo, which I still, to this day, years after doing my wine exams, find faintly amusing.

The steep slopes and terraced vineyards of the Douro are not tractor-friendly, so much of the picking is done by hand rather than machine. In fact, the grapes are often crushed by foot (mine included, once. It really is harder work than you'd imagine). This grape juice needs lots of colour and tannin extracted from the skins before it's fermented so that the resulting wine is deep in colour and texture; crushing the grapes by foot is an extremely effective way of doing this.

The wine is then fortified with a neutral-tasting grape spirit up to a heady 19–22 per cent alcohol by volume before being transferred into wooden barrels to begin the ageing process. ('Ageing process' sounds so much better than just 'getting old'. Might have to borrow that one.) This is where the style of port is determined into one of the following basic categories: white, ruby and tawny.

White port

This is port made with white grapes rather than red. They are fairly neutral in style, but have their place, namely in a glass with lots of tonic, a slice of lemon and a big bowl of salted almonds.

Ruby port

This is an inexpensive introduction to port and gives you the sweet, alcoholic mulberry (as in fruit, not handbag) kiss that port is famous for. Deep in colour, as the name suggests, and aged for no more than three years in stainless-steel vats or barrels.

Vintage port

This is ruby port, but one made from a single year and aged for around two years in barrels. It has to be an exceptional year for it to be declared a vintage year. The grapes have to reach optimum ripeness to make the cut for vintage port and, once the wine is released in bottles, it usually still needs ageing for *years* (anything between five and fifty, but usually around fifteen to twenty years as a rule) before it's anywhere near ready to drink.

The fortified wine inside the bottle will 'throw' sediment in the bottle, meaning you'll have loads of bits floating in your glass, unless it's decanted before pouring. This is because the wine isn't filtered before it's bottled, so it really is the dregs. Harmless though they are, you don't want to drink them. Like drinking coffee when the filter hasn't worked properly, it makes the liquid feel gritty. To decant the wine, take the bottle (which hopefully has been stored on its side in a cool place) and turn it upright the day before you want to drink it. Then carefully decant it, keeping back the last bit of wine with the sediment in the bottle. You could pour it through an old baby's muslin if you want, but given the state of mine I prefer a steady hand.

It'll stay in great condition for a couple of days, but after that the wine will start to deteriorate.

Late-bottled vintage

Known as LBV, this is a funny category of port. It's made from grapes from a single year (the same as vintage port, described above), but unlike vintage, it is then aged in wood for about four to six years before being bottled and released, ready to drink. In style, they are lighter than vintage and not nearly as complex, but they can be a good cheaper alternative if vintage is your thing.

Tawny

As the name suggests, this port is tawny in colour; amberhued, if you like. The idea is that tawny port is aged in wood for longer than ruby port, so the colour lightens with age.

The main thing to remember is that whereas proper vintage port needs further ageing in the bottle before it's ready to drink, tawny port is ready to go. Because the wines are slightly oxidized by the time you get them, due to time spent in wooden casks with a little exposure to air (see page 60 for an explanation of oxidation), they will last longer once opened than a vintage port.

Inexpensive tawny port makes a great pre-prandial, served very chilled, though aged tawnies (the age is indicated on the label) are more exciting, and their inherent dried-fruit-and-nut sweetness smells like Christmas in a glass.

Then there is Colheita, which is tawny port made from grapes from a single outstanding year and aged in wood for more than seven years. Expensive, but sublime, especially with crème brûlée. That's another one for the wine-drinking bucket list.

Sauternes

Having said all that, in my opinion, a sweet white Sauternes with its finely balanced sweetness and acidity is as brilliant a match for stilton as port, so you might as well try both and keep back a bit of Sauternes for pudding.

✱ SWEET STUFF

The flavours of Christmas pudding are so full on and so sweet, you need something equally unctuous to match it or it hasn't got a hope of peeping through the flavours in the dish. As just mentioned, Sauternes or the decadent Hungarian sweetie Tokaji are up to the task.

When it comes to chocolate, some swear by red wine as a great match (for more on that, see page 102), but by the time I've got to the Quality Street tin I'm usually on the Amaretto. And don't forget, if you need a little pick-me-up before bed, you've still got a bit of something sparkling left in the fridge. Pep it up with a dash of Campari and make it dirty.

In the old days, we'd have a second wind and the Husband would whip up a round of Brandy Alexanders (cream, Brandy and Crème de Cacao with a grating of nutmeg), but now he's too busy building various toys found in children's pillowcases. Serves him right.

NEW YEAR'S EVE

By New Year's Eve, I'm feeling fat, broke and socially done in. And so it was that we stopped doing New Year's Eve after the third baby arrived. Just. Too. Tired. But over the last few years, we've slowly collected a crowd of NYE regulars, a mixture of old friends staying with parents nearby and a few new ones. The first year we numbered ten, the next year fifteen, and by the following year word got round that we were running the NYE equivalent of a soup kitchen for knackered parents and we were up to twenty guests. Then we had a year off but, essentially, it made us realize that catering for a crowd doesn't have to be expensive or exhausting. First off, make it bring a bottle. I'm so over wine by then, I'm not too worried what I drink, and it usually tastes better when it's free. Food is usually a big piece of roasted meat or an enormous stew. One of the regulars does cheese and, for pudding, I make a really simple white chocolate mousse, always. Drinks-wise, it goes like this:

1. **Moscow Mules** on arrival (vodka, fresh lime juice and ginger beer).
2. **Wine** – whatever the guests bring, although I do tell them what we're eating in advance so they can pick something they think might go, and we'll throw in a couple of bottles too, Christmas leftovers . . .

3. **Fizz** for midnight – it's got to be the real stuff
   to see in the New Year. A good, solid Brut
   Non-Vintage, something tried and tested.

Quantities are more conservative given that we don't usually
see in the dawn nowadays, but we count on a couple of
Moscow Mules each, plus half a bottle of wine and a few
glasses of fizz per head over the whole evening. I'm aware
this probably falls into the category of binge drinking, but
it is New Year's Eve and we're about to go on the wagon
for a month – OK, a week (more on that next) – so I think
it's OK given the circumstances.

Time to go cold turkey. And I'm not talking sandwiches.

WHAT MAKES A WINE SUITABLE – OR NOT – FOR VEGETARIANS OR VEGANS?

Ever seen the words 'Suitable for Vegans' on a
bottle of wine and wondered what's in there to
make it unsuitable in the first place? After all, we're
talking about a bottle full of squashed, fermented
grapes. So far, so vegan.

But as part of the winemaking process most wines
are 'fined' to get any sediment out. We're talking
yeasts, bits of grape skin or pulp, that kind of thing.

As well as removing any unwanted particles, it also stabilises the wine so it won't develop any unwanted smells or tastes once in the bottle.

Thing is – and I don't mean to put you off your glass of wine – it's the stuff that's used to fine a wine in the first place that determines whether it'll be vegetarian- or vegan-friendly, or not. Fining agents, as they're called, include casein, which is milk-based or albumen, otherwise known as egg whites. Then there's isinglass (made from fish) or gelatin, another animal by-product. After fining the wine is then usually filtered but point is, the fining agent used might not be suitable for vegetarians or vegans in the first place.

However, lots of wines are fined using bentonite, a type of clay, or even synthetic fining agents. And some wines aren't fined or filtered at all, the winemaker preferring to leave it as it is. As it stands there's no legal requirement for wine producers to state whether a wine is suitable for vegetarians or vegans on the label. In fact, look at most wine labels and you won't find a list of ingredients. The only thing you might see ingredients-wise is 'contains sulphites', telling you that sulphur has been added to keep the wine fresh in the bottle (see page 211 for more on that). But more producers are now stating whether their wines are suitable or not on their wine labels and plenty of retailers include this information on their websites so that you can now search their sites specifically for them. But are they any good in the first place?

Well, yes. And no. Being vegetarian or vegan isn't a measure of quality; there are good and bad. And likewise just because a wine is organic (meaning that it's made from grapes grown without the use of synthetic fertilizers, fungicides, pesticides and herbicides in the vineyard) it doesn't mean it'll be suitable for vegans. I know. It's enough to give you a headache before you've even opened the bottle. (Talking of headaches, some are convinced that drinking vegan wines doesn't give you a headache. I wish I could say that's true but: alcohol. No matter if the wine is organic, vegan-friendly, natural or low in sulphur. If there's alcohol in there, drink too much and it's going to give you a headache.)

Most supermarkets now stock a fairly good range, there are lots more online retailers actively promoting them. Thankfully more wine labels are stating whether what's inside the bottle is suitable or not.

CHAPTER

EIGHT

BOOZE-FREE DAZE

'A day without wine is like a day without sunshine.' Or so a tea towel given to me at Christmas (not in the pillowcase, mind) tells me. How very true that is, apart from the time just after Christmas and New Year, when I feel like I've had rather too much sun, if you see what I mean. Everything about January screams abstinence, after the relative food/drink/present binge of December. In fact, compared to the velvet comfort of December, January feels positively jute-like.

I'm not really one for New Year's resolutions, mainly because I am more of an 'everything in moderation, including moderation' kind of woman. That, and I know I won't stick to them. One year I did give up trashy magazines for fear that my habit had got out of control. I used to dip in and out; one week *Hello!*, the next *Grazia*, the following week *OK!* My knowledge on high-street fashion, royals and Cheryl Cole was impressive. But before I knew it, I was doing all three in one week. So I went cold turkey and stopped buying them altogether, for a whole year. This led me to binge, mostly on visits to the hairdresser and often in the supermarket magazine aisle. Now I like to think I have found a balanced approach: *Vogue* and *Hello!* once a month. I can do without the inside track on soap stars, but fashion and Royals? *That* I need to know.

For many of us, January is the time when booze is given the heave-ho for the whole month. Or, in my case, a whole week. Yes, I know, not very impressive, but I don't drink like I used to. Parenting with a hangover is just too painful. That, and on top of all the health stuff my tolerance level is significantly lower than it used to be (such a cheap date), it's fattening and too much wine means I have a dreadful night's sleep and look about 106 years old the next day. I know I'm not alone. Social media is awash with conversations between mums who know that wine is not really the answer when you're tired and stressed. Chocolate is much better. But as with chocolate, so it is with wine. A little of the good stuff is usually better than lots of rubbish.

Apart from January, the only other time I have gone willingly completely wine-free is when pregnant. That said, I have usually found out about my pregnancies having had an evening in the weeks leading up to it involving a number of cocktails (not directly related to *why* I got pregnant, of course). Cue much guilt and worry about what a couple of Americanos might mean for my unborn baby. Then followed months of feeling sick at the mere thought of wine. But at about five months, I did have the odd glass of wine each week. I remember my doctor telling me a couple of small glasses a week was OK, and to use my common sense. So I did. And funnily enough, I didn't really miss it much. I think I was distracted by the constant indigestion and needing a wee at least twenty times a day. Hopefully the grown-up soft drinks below might provide inspiration when wine is not an option.

While we're on the subject, it seems like a good time to talk about how we teach our children about alcohol. Bear with me. A survey by the drinks industry-funded Drinkaware highlighted that only 17 per cent of adults had planned a 'dangers of alcohol' talk with their children. It made me think: how young is too young? Should they be shielded or gently shown the way with all things booze-related? It puts our own grown-up relationship with the bottle under the spotlight and that can make for uncomfortable viewing. Some felt that it was totally inappropriate to teach children about alcohol before they reach university age. Others thought watered-down Rioja with beans on toast was the right way to go. I'm not convinced either way.

Clearly, we need to talk about it, to help children learn about the good, the bad and the ugly side of alcohol before they start experimenting. Wine was always part of any family meal when I was growing up; I just wasn't allowed any. It was there, on the table, in the parents' glasses, but it wasn't a big deal. Admittedly, my teenage years were pre-alcopops, but we did have Taboo and large grounds at school in which to get lost in the undercliffs on a Saturday afternoon. We only had one bottle between five of us; it was never going to take us to alcoholic Armageddon, but it definitely got us tipsy. The thought of my own children experimenting with alcohol fills me with horror, but I know that at some stage they will, and I'm probably not going to be there when it happens. So I have to ensure they know the dangers before it does.

As you know, I look forward to 'wine o'clock', that time when the children are in bed, silence falls and my mind turns to food, telly and – if I'm feeling really productive – a chapter of a book. I choose my wines carefully, trying different things every week. Little and often; wine should be a journey, not a journey's end. That's what I hope to teach my children. However, wine at around 12–14 per cent ABV and costing over a fiver a bottle is probably not going to be the drink of choice for young people experimenting with alcohol.

Looking at the coverage following the Drinkaware survey, it was all about mums on sofas holding glasses of wine (and looking much better than I do at the end of the day). The research was well-intentioned and aimed at an engaged audience. The real issue, however, is how to fix the problem of really cheap, strong drinks (particularly cider, lager and ridiculously cheap spirits) being so widely available to a generation of drinkers who may only ever know the ugly side of alcohol. That is a different conversation, and rather more uncomfortable. I just hope I can enthuse mine (when they are old enough, obviously) so that they see wine as something to be explored and enjoyed (in moderation, obviously), not just a means to an end.

NO WINE-ING

Now, the problem I have when having a wine-free week is that food without wine (and I'm talking evenings) is like food without salt. It's just a bit boring. One option is to pep up the food as much as possible with lots of chilli-flecked noodle soups and spicy curry dishes. Another is to try and make the non-wine drinks as interesting as possible. A glass of water with supper is just too depressing for January. My absolute favourite non-alcoholic drink is ginger beer, which manages to be refreshing, exciting and all without a drop of alcohol. The shelves are now full of wondrous non-alcoholic drinks, but the problem is the nice ones aren't cheap and the cheap ones are full of sugar. Luckily, tomato juice isn't, so a good recipe for a virgin Bloody Mary is essential, along with a few more:

✳ VIRGIN BLOODY MARY

One carton of tomato juice, chilled; lime juice; lemon juice; pinch of celery salt; twist of black pepper; tiny pinch of cinnamon; and a slug of chilli oil. Mix all the ingredients, except the tomato juice, together in a large jug. Add the juice, stir and keep in the fridge. Drink that evening.

✳ MINT LEMONADE

Get a handful of mint, place a tea towel on top and bash gently with a rolling pin. Put it in a pitcher and pour over 3 tablespoons of sugar syrup (which you can either buy or make simply by boiling equal amounts of water and sugar together). Add the juice of up to six lemons, the zest of half those and top up with sparkling mineral water.

✳ CUCUMBER SPARKLE

Take a jug, pour in a bottle of sparkling water, add a dash of lemon or lime juice (or both, if you're in need of a citrus boost). Stick in a few sprigs of mint, a pinch of sea salt if you want it savoury, or a little bit of sugar syrup (boil water, add sugar, wait until dissolved) for a sweeter drink. Add loads of ice and then, yup, a cucumber. Either slice it fine or go chunky style, depending on mood, time and how cucumber-y you want it. Thinly sliced gives more flavour.

✳ POMEGRANATE PUNCH

Apparently, pomegranate juice increases the sex drive in both men and women, so go carefully on this unless you want an October baby. This is two parts pomegranate juice to one part sparkling water. Put it in a tumbler with ice and a bit of lemon rind to make it look like a proper grown-up drink and not just juice.

✳ MRS MILLS' ELDERFLOWER CORDIAL

This recipe was given to me by one of the mothers from school. One day, as I passed her on the way home, I saw Mrs Mills rummaging around in the hedgerow. Thinking she'd lost something, I stopped to ask if everything was OK. 'Oh yes,' she cried, 'elderflower heads!' And so it was that she gave me the recipe for home-made elderflower cordial, assuring me it was foolproof. Luckily, she was right. The only thing that foxed me was the citric acid, but she gave me some of hers.

You need twenty-five to thirty elderflower heads; zest and juice of three lemons and one orange; 1kg of sugar and 1 heaped teaspoon of citric acid. Add sugar to 1.5 litres of water, boil to dissolve. Remove from the heat and add citric acid. Put into a large bowl and add the fruit and flowers (heads of flowers only, no stems). Cover and leave for four days, stirring each day. Filter through muslin and squeeze the fruit, then pop into sealed bottles. It will keep for a few weeks at least, longer if you put them into sterilized bottles.

✳ AFFOGATO

OK, so this is technically more of a pudding than a drink, but it's absolutely delicious nonetheless and not an alcohol unit in sight. Take a glass and put two scoops of vanilla ice cream in. Next, prepare a shot of espresso coffee and pour it over. Eat it before it all melts and avoid sharing if possible.

WHAT MAKES A WINE LOWER IN ALCOHOL?

If you don't want to go completely booze-free but like the idea of drinking significantly lower-alcohol wines (wines with less than 9 per cent ABV), there are a growing number of wines available, made in different ways.

The first is by picking the grapes early, when sugar levels are lower than they might reach if left to ripen, and as sugar is fermented to alcohol (remember that bit? What did you come into the room for again?), lower sugar will mean lower alcohol in the resulting wine. However, picking the grapes early means acidity levels will be higher than if the grapes were picked later, which is fine as long as you are in the mood for crisp, rather than ripe fruity wine.

Another way to achieve naturally lower alcohol levels is to stop the fermentation before it has completely finished naturally. Again, this means lower resulting alcohol, but it also means higher natural sweetness as there is more sugar left in the wine. So you get lower alcohol but more sweetness. There is a third way, and that is removing some if not all of the alcohol from the wine. Progress is a wonderful thing, and we now have the technology to do this via various machines, but the quality of these wines varies enormously.

Some taste like wine, just not as we might know it. Light but not that fresh and definitely lacking in flavour, which isn't what I'm after. But some of these wines are getting better all the time, so I'll keep trying.

In the meantime, you could add water, or soda, and make a spritzer. If I'm going to have a lovely, light glass of wine I look for grape varieties that are able to produce wines with alcohol levels below 12 per cent, naturally. More about these in chapter fourteen; not here, because we're temporarily wine-free, remember?

CHAPTER
NINE

BOOK-CLUB WINES

know one shouldn't judge a book by its cover, but I do think you can tell a lot about someone by the books on their shelf. My bookshelves read like chapters of my life. I still have copies of beloved books from my childhood, such as *The Magic Faraway Tree* and *Malory Towers*. They then give way to the forbidden *Forever* by Judy Blume, which was passed around the classroom and read behind the flipped-up tops of wooden desks, out of sight of the teachers. The name Ralph has never been quite the same for me. Then there was *Lace* – 'Which one of you bitches is my mother?' – obviously. My later teens were dominated by school-influenced reads, including the obligatory obsession with Plath and Hardy. My friend Pudding (nickname, thankfully) and I once refused to read Milton, resulting in a class stand-off with Mr Stubbs, my beloved English teacher. He won, but just the thought of that text still makes me shudder.

I peppered this period with Binchy and Wesley (Maeve and Mary) just to stop my head from exploding. My twenties were dominated by awkward books with weird titles in a bid to make myself more clever and interesting (it didn't work), and my thirties were marked by parenting books to make myself a better parent (it didn't work). Then I ran out of steam. Instead of reaching for a book at night, I would read a magazine. In my frazzled state, it was all I could cope with. Then the addiction got out of hand, as you know. That's when book club came along and saved me.

I remember thinking that I would never be in a book club. After years of being told what to read at school, the very idea of being told what to read as an adult seemed ridiculous. Little did I know that one day, book club would be one of those evenings I looked forward to more than any other, not least because nights out during the week are a rare and beautiful thing.

The founding member of our book club was Madeleina. Now, this is not her real name, but when I told my book club that I was writing a book, the thing they got most excited about was their book-club name, one that would make them sound more exotic and, well, literary. So, from now on, please note that * denotes a book-club name. Anyway, Madeleina* had just moved to the area after years of living in the city and missed her old book club, so she emailed a few friends one day with a date and a title. She's a fairly decisive kind of woman, the sort who could probably sort out Europe in between helping an elderly neighbour in with her shopping.

Our first meeting was a bit like a first date, with everyone being fairly polite and not wanting to upset anyone by dissing the book. Nowadays, you could say we have relaxed into each other's company. In other words, we know each other well enough to spot when someone has skim-read a book just to look good. I'm not a natural skim-reader, I have to read every word, and often reread them if I've forgotten what I've just read. In fact, this explains my love of a good Jilly Cooper novel, as she puts a list of characters in the front of her books. I can read and reread away, and when I've forgotten who's married to/having an affair with/illegitimately fathered who, I can go back and check the cast list at the front. Genius.

Most of the time the books divide opinion: Steinbeck's *The Grapes of Wrath* being a classic example. Whereas it made Swallow* (who wanted to call her daughter this if she'd had one; thankfully she's got four boys) weep at the bit about hunger in the stomachs of your children, it made me want to throw the book at the wall. Too. Much. Dust. Most were unmoved by the cupcake novel – sweet and fluffy inside, but ultimately not that nourishing – whereas Madeleina* wanted to burn it right there and then. Denny (real name, she's a realist) skipped through the one about Middle Eastern politics in between night shifts at the hospital. That one made me flee to an illicit Jilly Cooper for comfort. Pandora* hated the one written by the American guy who was obsessed with sex (and wrote about

it terribly), whereas I found it weirdly amusing. Saffron*
loved the literati one; Domino* was reminded – not in a
good way – of an old boyfriend by the one about the two
hapless climbers in 1950s Afghanistan. And it turns out
Tyger* loves a thriller. The one to unite us all in pure joy
was Nancy Mitford's *The Pursuit of Love*. Oh! How we
sighed.

Within the group, past and present professions include
psychology, medicine, law, journalism and 'various'. All of
us have very different lives to those we had before children
– twenty-two children between us at last count. What unites
us – other than being mothers – is a love of getting round
a table and talking, listening, laughing, swearing, arguing,
agreeing, sharing. I say sharing: Madeleina* used to work
with a Really Famous Person, and as much as I try to get
her to share information, annoyingly she's far too discreet.
I'm working on that.

Anyway, it is she who ensures we discuss the book for at
least part of the evening, but it is by no means the only
topic of conversation. An example of one evening's discussion
topics went something like this: magnificent bosoms (not
ours); poorly children (ours); euthanasia (generally); the
Mitford sisters (the book discussion part); newborn babies
(there was a three-week-old in attendance that night); *Marley
& Me* (– *tiny voice* – I loved it); the importance of Jilly
Cooper in one's life (as previously mentioned); and sperm
washing (I always learn *something* new).

On occasion, we have been known to all finish the book at the same time. Obviously, as mothers, we're all at a stage where reading time is hardly abundant, so if a book isn't working for me, I'll read something else. Once, having given up on a book two-thirds of the way through (the terribly written sex one – it got boring after a while), I reverted to bad habits and took a copy of a well-known weekly magazine as a diversion, knowing that I had little to say on the book but had done my homework on outfits worn to a particular royal wedding. One of the members, who shall remain nameless (Swallow*), clearly hadn't been near a magazine like that for years and, like a woman possessed, pored over every page, every outfit, every minor European royal, head down, oblivious to the doubtless deep and erudite discussion happening around her.

We might not all finish the book, but one of the things we've done from the very first meeting is make trying a new wine part of the evening. Whoever is hosting at their house, cooks. Originally, the idea was to keep it to fuss-free, low-maintenance food, but ever since someone (Swallow*, again) raised the bar with a home-made curry and dhal, there has been a steady culinary climb. Madeleina* tried to rein it in, but it fell on deaf ears. Clearly, we are tougher than Europe.

I always take a couple of bottles – one red, one white – of something unusual for people to try, not in a ceremonial make-a-big-deal-of-it way, but just as a glass to have over food while talking. And, as we go round the table discussing the book, so we talk about the wine. When we first did this, it felt a bit strange, discussing wine. But if we can assert our opinions on things like books, or food, why don't we feel as confident when it comes to wine? I suspect the reason is that we've been conditioned to associate certain words with wine-speak and so worry that we're not using the 'right' vocabulary, or that we might sound silly. But it really doesn't have to be this way. We should use whatever language we want.

In fact, sometimes actions say more than words, and a facial expression can be the best indicator of what someone really thinks of a wine. There's the wince (not good), the cheek-sucker (indicating acidity in the wine), and the lip-smacker (indicating more please). The point is everyone gets to try a wine they might not have tasted before and talk about it. By doing that, you can start to build up a memory bank of tastes and flavours, and start to explore what you like and don't like so much. By talking about it, even just a bit, you can build your confidence and extend your personal dictionary of words and range of cheek-sucking, lip-smacking facial expressions.

The problem is, to have a memory bank, you need a good memory, and the one thing I have noticed is that motherhood messes with one's memory. It certainly has with mine, anyway. I know it's a cliché, but I don't remember ever leaving my keys in the fridge before I had children. (I'm yet to leave my handbag in the chest freezer, as a friend's mother did, but I'm sure my time will come.) Or perhaps I did, and I just can't remember it.

With so many different grapes, countries and tastes to remember, it's sometimes useful to attach a specific characteristic to a particular flavour in order to give the memory a nudge in the right direction. Let's take leading men as an example: Benicio for Barolo (dark, brooding), Clooney for modern Riojas (gets increasingly better with age). As for Don Draper, he would have to be a Chilean Merlot: smooth but not quite what it seems (for years, what they thought was Chilean Merlot was actually another grape altogether, Carmenère. Over time, he/it has been exposed for what he/it really is). Here I give you grapes by literary genre. Depending on what you're in the mood for, there's a grape to match it:

Genre	Grape
Bonnet buster	Gewürztraminer: white grape, floral with a bit of spice
Crime	Malbec: red grape, dark, broody and a little bit dangerous
Fantasy (more *Lord of the Rings* than *Fifty Shades of Grey*)	Chardonnay: white grape, can morph into many things depending on what the winemaker wants to create
History	Muscat: the world's oldest grape variety, can make dry whites or sweet whites, as well as sparkling wines
Horror	Pinotage: a red grape grown in South Africa, not for the faint-hearted

Genre	Grape
Literary prizewinner	Riesling: the ethereal grape, sometimes difficult to get your head round
Poetry	Pinot Noir: red grape, smooth and silky, beautiful when good, can bring tears to the eyes
Politics	Semillon: a white grape, sometimes fruity, sometimes oily. Like politicians
Light romance	Torrontés: from Argentina, fresh, light and floral
Dark romance	Cabernet Sauvignon: red grape, black fruits, sometimes spicy
Sci-fi	Pinot Grigio: actually technically a black grape, not white. The skin, that is. Weird

When it comes to tasting and talking about wine, book club is an ideal, informal setting in which to do it. But sometimes it's worth doing it properly, with more than a few wines in front of you so that you can really compare and contrast different styles of wine. Taste a Sauvignon Blanc next to a Chardonnay; or a New World Chardonnay next to a wine from Chablis (also made from the Chardonnay grape but the latter is normally unoaked). Try a Rioja next to an unoaked red to see what oak does to a wine, or a Prosecco next to a Champagne to compare what bubbles in a bottle do when made in different ways from different countries, with different grapes and different resulting sweetness. But even if you only have one wine in front of you, make time to taste it.

When you are tasting wines side by side like this, it really is worth having a couple of empty glasses in front of you. That way you can pour one, try it, pour another and compare it. By trying wines side by side, you can really stick your nose in, work the taste buds and see the differences in the wines. We so rarely do this, as most of us only have one glass of wine on the go at any time. My mother, on the other hand, has several, mostly because she can never remember where she put her glass down. Anyway, more than one glass if possible and, even better, a blank sheet of white paper so that you can look at the colour of the wine against a white background (it sounds a bit OTT, but it does make a big difference when you are looking at two wines side by side).

At book club, we'll have a few wines on the go and usually share glasses, but when I'm doing wine tastings for people choosing what to serve at a big party, we'll usually taste up to eight wines side by side, so the best wine can win. They will be tasted blind (as in, the bottles are covered up so those choosing don't know which wine is which) and I've learnt from experience to number the glasses so as to avoid – in the words of the Fat Controller – confusion and delay. Doing it 'blind' means that price and place do not affect judgement, you are really left to concentrate on the smells, tastes and flavour. And there is nearly always a clear winner, often not the cheapest but rarely the most expensive either. On which we'll have more in a couple of chapters' time.

BOOK-CLUB WINE COURSE

One idea is to organize your book club to bring different wines to each meeting and to do comparative tastings each time you meet, tasting different wines side by side so that you can really see the differences. You don't need to bring a bottle each, obviously, so you could take it in turns and spread the cost. Here's a suggested running order:

✳ MEETING 1 – FIZZ

1 x bottle of Prosecco
1 x bottle of Champagne

Taste them side by side, compare the bubbles, the aromas and the flavours. See how many prefer the softer, sweeter Prosecco style to the crisper, more complex Champagne style.

✳ MEETING 2 – SAUVIGNON BLANC

1 x bottle of New Zealand Sauvignon Blanc
1 x bottle of Sancerre

Same grape, different countries. Notice how much the place impacts the flavour of the grape.

✳ MEETING 3 – CHARDONNAY

1 x bottle of Australian Chardonnay
1 x bottle of Chablis

Same grape, different countries. Again, see how much place, and winemaking, impacts the flavour.

✳ MEETING 4 – OFF-ROAD WHITES

1 x bottle of Argentinian Torrontés
1 x bottle of Chilean Viognier
1 x bottle of German dry Riesling

And now for something completely different. Just look at how exciting life beyond Chardonnay, Sauvignon and Pinot Grigio can be!

✳ MEETING 5 – JUICY REDS

1 x bottle of Beaujolais Villages (it will be made from the Gamay grape)
1 x bottle of Chilean Merlot

This one is all about juicy fruit and soft tannins. Again, contrast Old World with New and different grape varieties.

✳ MEETING 6 – SPICY REDS

1 x bottle of French Syrah (from the Rhône, a blend if necessary)
1 x bottle of South African Pinotage

Again, different countries and different grapes, but feel the tannins at work here. Warning: you'll need food with flavour for this one, something like a chilli or spicy stew.

This is only an introduction, but with a bit of forward planning you could bring so many different regions and grape varieties to the table. Just don't forget to talk about the book you've all been reading (or often not quite finished in my case) at some point.

CAN YOU JUDGE A WINE BY ITS LABEL?

Imagine buying a pair of shoes without trying them on. Oh, most of you have done that. OK, how about ordering a pizza and asking the waiter to put whatever he wants on it? You wouldn't, unless you are the kind of ker-ay-zee person who'll risk having to pay for and consume something you might not like, though you won't know that you don't like it until you've tried it, by which time you'll have paid for it and won't be able to get your money back. See where I'm going?

Buying wine can be a game of chance, but it can be made easier by knowing what to look for on the label and how to spot the signs that will point you in the right direction. The first things to look for include where the wine is made and what grape variety, or varieties, it's made from. Unlike wine from the New World, Old World wines often don't have a grape variety stated on the front label. You are supposed to just *know* that Chablis is made from Chardonnay, red Burgundy is made from Pinot Noir and Rioja is made from Tempranillo. Luckily, the idea of helping us find what we like has caught on and it's becoming more common to find a reference to the grape somewhere on the back label.

Vintage is another sign. If a wine has a year on it, the wine is made from grapes picked that year, that is, 'the vintage'. It's telling you the year the harvest happened. Some wine doesn't have a year on it, because it's made from a blend of grapes from different years. Champagne is a good example here, with the letters NV (standing for Non Vintage) shown proudly on the label. Because, in Champagne, blending is an art form and the aim is for each 'house' or producer to create a style of wine that doesn't change from year to year for their signature non-vintage blend. So, having a vintage on the label doesn't automatically mean it is better than one without; it depends on the wine.

Wines that do list the vintage, however, are sometimes shouting about their differences from previous years. Port is an example of how vintage is everything. With port, not every year is deemed good enough to be 'declared' – meaning the port houses decide whether it's a good enough year to shout about – as a vintage year, hence all the fuss about vintage port. Remember, older doesn't always mean better. If you want a really fresh, crisp, fruity dry white or rosé, then usually the younger the better. For inexpensive juicy ripe reds too, youth is good.

As we've already established, one shouldn't judge a book by its cover, but I do think that a good guide is the look of the label. If a wine producer has bothered to have a good-looking label made for their wine then it shows they're making an effort. Of course, there are exceptions: I have tried bottles with a nice-enough label and found a horror within. Equally, a horrible label might contain a gem of a wine. However, a good rule of thumb is, if they've taken time with the label, they care about what you think.

Your best bet when it comes to labels is to look at the story on the back label. What has the producer decided to tell you? What the wine tastes like? What food to match it with? If there is good information on the back label then again, the producer (or the shop selling you the wine) is at least making an effort to help you. I like that. It doesn't *always* work, but it is a good indicator.

TRUE OR FALSE? THE AGE OF A WINE IS AN INDICATION OF QUALITY

Just as the age of a mum is not necessarily an indication of quality (in fact, I think my standards are slipping, I am just *too* tired), so the age of a wine is not necessarily an indication of quality. Of course, there are lots of wines that are made to be aged and will improve if left to 'age' in the bottle. However, the majority of wines made today are made to be drunk within the year, perhaps two at a push. White wines especially: the younger they are drunk the better, as the delicate aromas and fruit flavours will develop over time, but not in a good way. In fact, they will lose the best thing about them: their freshness.

Red wines, especially those aged in oak, are made to age and have tannin in their structure, which provides the backbone to allow them to age gracefully, and hopefully develop into a more interesting wine over time. The nightmare is, there is no way of knowing how a wine is ageing in the bottle, apart from cracking it open and drinking it. If you have a case of a particular wine, this isn't a problem; if the wine still tastes too young, too tight, just leave it for a while – another six months, another year – before coming back and trying another bottle. But if you have just the one bottle – bad luck! If you are spending big money on investment wines, they will improve over decades. You'll just have to be patient. And then invite me for dinner.

CHAPTER

TEN

HALF-TERM HOLS

Let's discuss art. So, by now, halfway through the school year, I can't see much of my fridge any more. This is owing to the enormous amount of various children's random artwork stuck to it. That and letters about things I have to remember to send the kids to school with (as if just getting them all into the car on time every morning isn't enough of a challenge).

Here's the thing: does *not* putting up every single piece of artwork that comes back from school on the fridge make one a bad mother? I like to think not. Why, then, do I feel so bad when something doesn't make it onto the fridge? And at what point do you actually throw the stuff out? Of course, I have favourite bits that will never, ever be got rid of. Each of their first-ever pictures (at least the ones that count as a drawing as opposed to random scribblings) are framed and hang on the wall in the kitchen. It's all the stuff in between I worry about.

Artwork goes on the fridge for a time and then, when it gets to the stage that the whole lot blows off every time the back door is opened because each magnet is holding up *at least* four bits of paper, I cull. At night, once the children are in bed. I think I'm afraid that if they see me get rid of a single piece of artwork it will scar them for life. Tell me I'm not alone.

Anyway, the amount of artwork on the fridge is directly related to where we are in the school year, and by now we're well in. As are you and your work at wine school. Your half-term homework is to look at white wines, having done reds before Christmas. Here's a reminder of how white wine is made:

Pick grapes

Crush

Press

Ferment

Mature (sometimes in oak barrels)

Bottle

So, largely the same process as for red wine, but with one big difference: the grapes are crushed and pressed before fermentation and the juice is not fermented with the skins, unlike red wine, when it's fermented with the skins. The reason being that the skins are where the colour is, and we're talking white wine here. As you know, white wine can be so light in colour as to look almost like water, and it can also be much darker, like your wee when you're pregnant (or is that just me)? Whilst we are on the subject, can I just point out how completely ridiculous it is to expect a heavily pregnant woman, who can't see over her bump, to fill a tiny test tube with wee? When I think of the time spent in the loo at midwife appointments, trying desperately not to *pee all over my hand* . . .

Anyway, as I was saying, this difference in colour is because, although the juice is clear, grape varieties with thicker skins will have more colour in them. The resulting white wine will depend on the grape colour and how long the juice is left in contact with the skins once the grapes are crushed. The thing about white wine is that it's more delicate than red. It doesn't have the colour or tannins to fall back on; it's more about freshness, fruit and acidity. Winemakers need to be extra careful about keeping the juice clean and fresh, and away from air so that oxidation of the juice (and after fermentation, the wine) is avoided.

There are a couple of other things worth noting about white wine that we don't worry about so much with red wine. The first is whether the wine goes through a natural process called malolactic fermentation. This happens naturally after the first fermentation and it converts the sharper apple-like acids in the wine (the malo acids) to softer milk-like acids (lactic acids). The process softens the wine, making it less noticeably acidic, and the winemaker can choose whether he wants this to happen or not. A good example is ripe, almost creamy, buttery Chardonnay wines from Australia; they've usually been through malolactic fermentation.

Another big influencing factor is whether the wine has had any lees contact. Lees is basically sediment, made up of dead yeast and skins that may be left in contact with the wine in the barrel or tank for a short time after fermentation. This adds a certain texture to the wine, giving it an almost bread-like smell. If you can, try a Muscadet Sur Lie from the Loire Valley in France, this will show you what I mean. Made from the Melon de Bourgogne grape, you can buy Muscadet made with or without lees contact. 'Sur Lie' is, literally, 'on the lees'. It can be gorgeous; try it, preferably when it's sunny and you have a huge plate of delicious seafood in front of you.

ROSÉ-TINTED GLASSES

And then there is rosé wine. Made like a white wine, treated by winemakers as a white wine and treated by us as a joyful thing not to be taken too seriously. Which is good. And bad. The problem is, the cheap, sweet 'Blush' wine from California and the cheap, sweet stuff in funny-shaped bottles from Portugal has given rosé a bit of a reputation, and I'm not talking quality.

In fact, rosé wines have enjoyed something of a winemaking revolution in recent years, when more of us started drinking it and wine producers started making better rosés. Think of the beautiful pale-pink rosé wines from the South of France. Or the lovely jewel-like hot pinks from the Navarra region in Spain, or from Chile or Argentina; so many good pinks to choose from!

Rosé wine is not a joke. Rather, it is a joy. It gets its colour from being left in contact with the skins of the grapes for a short time (anything from a few hours to a few days), so obviously it needs to be made from grapes with a bit of colour on the skins. Because of that skin contact, there is a little bit of tannin as well as colour in the resulting wine.

Some of the most delicious rosé wines around at the moment are made from the red grape Garnacha (in Spain) or Grenache (in France) – same grape, different name. Grenache is one of the grapes often used in the beautiful pale-pink rosé wines made in Provence, where half the rosé in France comes from. Drink it with a tomato salad drenched in dressing and you'll find happiness, I swear.

There is another method of getting colour into rosé, and that is bleeding, otherwise known in France, much more romantically I must say, as the 'saignee' method. Here, a portion of red grape juice is taken after just a short period in contact with the skins, so there is just a bit of colour, not a lot. You can, if you want to, just add some red wine to white wine and make it pink, but by law you can't do this in France, except in Champagne.

In summary, avoid the sweet stuff (not least because it doesn't really taste of wine) and get aboard the pink train. Oh, the places you'll go!

ORANGE WINES

Well, more amber than orange but whatever, this is another whole (colour)way to enjoy wines made from white grapes. What makes them different is they're made like a red wine. So, instead of the juice of the grapes being separated from the skins before the wine is fermented, the juice and skins are left together for days, weeks or months, even years. The juice then takes on colour from the skins, turning it every shade from pale amber to deep orange.

You're more likely to find them on trendy restaurant wine lists than on supermarket shelves but there are a growing number of good, relatively inexpensive ones to be found. Having said that, there's nothing new about them. Orange wines date back thousands of years in Georgia, where they were made and aged in large clay pots called qvevri (pronounced kev-ree). White grapes were pressed and left to ferment – juice, skins, pips, stems and all – in the qvevri, then sealed and buried in the ground to keep the temperature cool and constant. In Slovenia and northern

Italy, white wines have been fermented with their grape skins for centuries too but a more recent resurgence of interest in the style has seen white-made-as-red wines popping up in places like Canada, Australia, South Africa – even England. The people that make them are usually making wines on a fairly small-scale, often working with organically grown grapes and using little or no added sulphur once the wines are made.

So what do they taste like? Well, a good one manages to combine the freshness of a white wine with the depth of a red, with flavours of stone fruits, nuts and often something a little herbal to it. There's texture and a definite grip to the wines too thanks to tannins from the skins being taken up by the juice when left together. And with their savoury flavours and bone-dry freshness, they're brilliantly food-friendly too. When it comes to serving them, treat it as you would a red. So, keep it at (cool) room temperature unless it's a particularly warm day, in which case let it chill in the fridge for a short time before opening the bottle.

BACK TO WHITES

Let's have a look at the main white grapes, just to top up your grape knowledge. Think of it as more wine satnav programming. Preloading, in a good way.

✳ CHARDONNAY

A bit like reality TV stars, this grape pops up anywhere and everywhere it can. You can't escape it. It's one of the so-called 'noble' grape varieties. A better class of grape, if you like. I've heard lots of people say that they don't like Chardonnay without realizing that it's the grape behind great white Burgundy wines, including Chablis. I suspect these same people have been left traumatized by an over-oaked Chardonnay at some point in their lives and therefore haven't returned to it in a hurry. However, the over-oaked Chardonnay style is less common now, thanks to changing tastes and responsive winemaking.

As a grape, it is relatively easy to grow and ripen, producing sizeable crops. The actual taste of the grape is pretty non-descript, but winemakers love the malleable character of Chardonnay. They can really play around and influence the end result with their winemaking trickery/alchemy. Chardonnay loves oak, and it changes character again when allowed to go through the natural 'second' malolactic fermentation process (which you now know about).

It may be ubiquitous, but Chardonnay comes in so many guises that there are enough differing styles to suit different tastes. It is also the white grape variety used to make Champagne (but you already knew that). Whether you want tropical fruit flavours, a peachy queen, a steely Chablis-style wine or even one with sparkles, there will be a Chardonnay for you. I've just got to help you find it.

✳ SAUVIGNON BLANC

I always think of Sauvignon Blanc as being a rather uptight grape. Basically, if any grape needed a drink, this one does. It's lean, linear and is behind the wines of Sancerre, so I know it can do posh. But think of New Zealand Sauvignon Blanc: more passion fruit than the nipped-in-at-the-waist, Sancerre-style Sauvignons. A style I love, in fact. Sauvignon Blanc used to fall into the floral – or herbaceous – category of descriptors, but Sauvignon Blanc is now more varied than ever. Nevertheless, if I stuck my nose into a glass and didn't get a hint of grass/lime/passion fruit, I would feel cheated.

✳ PINOT GRIGIO

This one first appeared in inexpensive, brightly lit pizza joints across the land, but soon spread from restaurant wine lists onto supermarket shelves and is now one of the most famous grape varieties of all. Italy is where much of it is grown, but given the success it's had, it's now found in almost every wine-growing country. Everyone's having a go. So, what does it taste like? Well, not an awful lot usually, but it does have an attractive quality: quaffability. Actually, I am being unfair. Try a Pinot Gris (same grape family) made in the Alsace region in France and all of a sudden there's much more happening in the glass. The same goes for one from Australia, or even New Zealand. Sadly, there'll be much less left in your wallet compared with the cheap-as-chips PG largely found in Italy, but at least you're likely to remember it long after you've forgotten the name of that cheap Italian one you bought on offer last week.

✳ RIESLING

I curtsey to a so-called 'noble' grape variety here. Say Riesling to people who take wine far too seriously and you'll see them go misty-eyed. Why the fuss? I have seen the word ethereal attached to it, but that's a cop-out. It's difficult to describe, but it goes something like this: lime fruit, mouthwatering acidity, floral notes, a hint of kerosene. Yes, I know I just described a wine as tasting like petrol, but as ever, stick some in your mouth, swish it about, suck in some air and swallow. Then think about what you can taste.

Germany is where you'll find some of the best Riesling wines in the world, but it's also where you'll find some of the worst. Go for the smarter stuff and you'll find that kerosene note. Perhaps I'll go with ethereal after all.

✳ SEMILLON

I don't often reach for the Semillon over the others. It's a funny beast – fruity but a little oily. I could be describing one of my mother's old boyfriends. Maybe that's why I can't get excited about it as a single grape variety. Australia's Hunter Valley produces some wonderful Semillon wines, but you've got to allow them time to develop and we're not very good at doing that any more. The longest a bottle of wine stays in our kitchen cupboard is a matter of weeks (unless it's been won in a school fête raffle, then it can stay there for *years*). No, where this grape hits its stride is when it's left to rot – actually, properly rot – on the vine, way past when everything else has been picked, and is used to make a sweet wine. Here, you don't want to stop the rot, or *Botrytis cinerea* to give it its proper name, because the juice left in the shrivelled grape is so concentrated and sweet, packed with natural sugars, as to be bacchanalian nectar.

Semillon is one of the grapes – the others are Sauvignon Blanc and Muscadelle – used in the making of Bordeaux's great sweet white, Sauternes. In Sauternes, one vine might produce as little as one small bottle of wine. Liquid gold.

✳ CHENIN BLANC

Alas, poor Chenin. It really is a good grape, making some of the finest sweet and dry wines in France, namely from the Loire Valley. However, the same variety is behind some of the cheapest and not-so-cheerful wines from elsewhere. Treated with love and care, Chenin Blanc can produce beautiful wines with rich lemon flavours and an almost honey-like character. Unloved, it can produce white wines that make one's mouth resemble a cat's backside. Not a good look, even by candlelight. Tread carefully and spend a little more than you would do normally and you'll probably be treated to everything that's good about Chenin. Pick up a bargain Chenin and, well . . . don't say I didn't warn you.

✳ GEWÜRZTRAMINER

A suitably fitting name for what is a mouthful of a wine. Gewürztraminer is a white grape often described as spicy and as such, fittingly, it matches up to gently spicy foods like Asian curries. Gewürz (as it's affectionately known by people who have pet names for grapes) is a spicy, floral number, and drinking it is not unlike drinking Turkish-delight-scented wine. Odd but delicious. It's one I'm not always in the mood for, but when I am I always wonder why I don't drink it more often. Not easy to quaff; it's a meal in a glass. Alsace in France is a great place to start your Gewürztraminer journey, with stop-offs in Chile and New Zealand.

✳ TORRONTÉS

This is a grape to watch. Not literally, obviously – that would be dull – what I mean is, interesting things are happening here. It's currently Argentina's calling card, if there is such a thing in white wine, and is making a mark thanks to its light, flowery aromas and easy citrus flavours. It's not expensive to produce but it must be drunk young in order to get that lovely freshness. Once it starts to develop in the bottle, it can lose that gorgeous fruit that makes it so delicious. You want this young and fresh.

✳ VIOGNIER

Viognier is a grape with attitude. It carries weight, produces wine with a fairly high alcohol content and packs a flavour punch. Mostly peach, sometimes orange, occasionally lemons; it's an overflowing fruit bowl. It is most famous as the white grape of the Rhône region and is often added to some of the great northern Rhône red wines (made from the Syrah grape) in dash-like proportions. I love it; it always feels round and ripe to me, like a rather lovely cuddle. It is usually fairly high in alcohol too, so make that a bear hug.

These are the classic, and a few not-so-classic, ones that make up our patchwork quilt of grape varieties, ready for you to preload. But, as we did with red wines, I want you to look beyond the grape varieties and have a look at the white-wine styles listed below. Make an effort to seek some of these out when you're next in the supermarket, local wine shop or online shopping.

Write them down in your swanky wine notebook, or just scrawl them in biro on the back of your hand (rub off if seeing anyone in authority, like, say, your child's teacher). Whevs, the point is to get off the beaten track without being put off by not really knowing what you're letting yourself in for. Go forage:

✳ SPANISH WHITES AND ROSÉS (THERE IS LIFE OUTSIDE RIOJA)

If you like clean, crisp, lemony whites, then you have to – HAVE TO – try an Albariño white. Albariño is a grape grown in the Rias Baixas region in north-west Spain and is very much flavour of the month when it comes to Spanish white wine. Lean and green, with lime fruit and almost ear-splitting acidity, this is a gorgeous spring/summer wine. Some find it too sharp (the Husband included), but happily that means more for me. Navarra is another region to look out for and is a pretty sure bet when looking for a bright, juicy, modern style of rosé. It's not a shy wine, full-bodied by rosé standards.

✳ SOUTHERN FRENCH WHITES (THERE IS LIFE OUTSIDE CHABLIS) –

The grape to look for here is Picpoul, meaning 'lip-stinger', apparently because of the high acidity of the grape. I promise you it doesn't sting. It does tingle, though. A good one will give you jasmine-scented aromas, peach-like fruit flavours and crisp acidity. Another one to look out for is Vermentino (the grape) from the Languedoc-Roussillon region. Also found in Italy, young Vermentino is what we'd be better off drinking instead of Pinot Grigio, if only we could find it. Sadly, you have to hunt for it. It's lemon-fresh and is exactly right for pasta and pesto (a staple in this house).

✳ ITALIAN WHITES MADE FROM UNPRONOUNCEABLE GRAPES

Although it sounds like it, Falanghina is not a sexual act. Rather, it is a grape I told you to put on your fridge-door white list back in chapter one. You say it like this: Falan-geen-ah. Hard 'g'. Made in southern Italy, largely in Campania, this is one of many brilliantly fresh and relatively uncomplicated Italian whites that can thrill with their simplicity and make you want to eat more. Another two to add to the list are the richer, riper Fiano (that's the name of the grape, also found in southern Italy) and the crisp, apple-like Greco di Tufo (Greco is the grape; Tufo, in Campania, is where it's made). That should keep you busy.

✳ CHILEAN WHITES FROM THE CASABLANCA VALLEY AND BEYOND

I absolutely love Chilean wines. When I started buying wine, Chile was all about Chardonnay and Cabernet Sauvignon grown in the huge Central Valley region. Then came the discovery of the Casablanca Valley wines, particularly Sauvignon Blanc. This northern region is generally cooler, with soils and sea breezes suited to ripening aromatic grapes like Sauvignon Blanc and Pinot Noir. Just south of the Casablanca Valley is the San Antonio Valley, another one to watch. Leyda is a region within San Antonio and the producers there are making some brilliant Sauvignon Blanc wines, crisp as a classic white shirt. Put it on your list of must-haves.

✳ NEW ZEALAND WHITES NOT FROM MARLBOROUGH

Yes, Marlborough Sauvignon Blanc can be lovely, really lovely. But it can also be *everywhere*, stopping you getting beyond it to anything else. So instead search out Pinot Gris from Marlborough, Chardonnay from Hawkes Bay and Sauvignon Blancs, Rieslings and even Gewürztraminers from the Martinborough region, east of Wellington in New Zealand's North Island. Having tasted hundreds of wines from here, all blind (as in the bottles were covered so I didn't know what they were), at an international wine competition, I can tell you that these were the ones that lit up my taste buds. They've got eye-wateringly good Pinot Noir too.

So, we're all white. And rosy-cheeked. Not only have we made it through half-term in one piece, you've done your homework on time too. Star pupils, the lot of you.

CHAPTER

ELEVEN

SUNDAY ROAST

There was a time when the Sunday papers were read cover to cover all before our first glass of wine at lunchtime on a Sunday. No longer. Now I might manage one article in short bursts over the course of the morning, in between feeding/dressing/conversing with various small people in the house. By the time dogs have been walked, lunch has been devoured and children/homework sorted, the Sunday slumber sets in and I've lost my appetite for all but the magazine bits. Maybe a bit of property porn at a push. But I can't imagine it any other way nowadays: it's all good (news).

Papers aside, I really do think nothing, *nothing* compares with the weekend meal that is a Sunday roast. There is something so glorious about putting food on the table for everyone to tuck in to. Hours in the preparation, minutes in the eating; it can be an awful lot of work, but it's always worth it. The roast is this greedy girl's dream. To be honest, as much as I would love to think I am a natural jus-making, appear-from-nowhere cook, I am not. I cook with precision, especially roasts. On the inside cover of my favourite, very battered cookbook is a list of timings for roasts, depending on what it is and when we are going to eat it (I told you I was a scary list lady).

Lunch usually means lunch, but on a day when one of the children has got an afternoon birthday party (on a Sunday! Why do that?) we go for the 5 p.m.-ish roast. It's pretty traditional fayre in this house: a roast chicken stuffed with garlic, lemon and herbs or a half leg of lamb roasted Mediterranean-style or beef with Yorkshires. Every now and again I try cooking pork, but I'm fated with it, always managing to completely dry it out, leaving it more than a little disappointing. There will be tons of potatoes (you'll see why in a minute) and extras like cauliflower cheese if I'm organized enough. While pudding is, without fail, ice cream, sometimes with chocolate brownies or a crumble in colder months.

As the cook, it is obligatory to have a glass of something on the go and a small bowl of crisps or olives within reach as I potter around the kitchen. It's usually a really cold glass of white first, switching to red when we eat. If I can justify it, then the white might have bubbles in it, but only if I'm sharing/feeling slightly reckless. I'll come on to what wine to put with what meat in a bit (we've already covered this in some detail in chapter six, but here is where we get into specifics).

GOOD THINGS TO QUAFF WHILE COOKING/NIBBLING

✳ FINO/MANZANILLA

Remember the store-cupboard essentials? Well, cleverly, you've already stocked up on a half-bottle of either Fino or Manzanilla to keep in your fridge door. This comes in useful now when you want to sip on something whilst cooking in the kitchen. Best matched with salted almonds or great big Spanish olives, preferably the ones stuffed with feta.

✳ A *COUPE DE CHAMPAGNE*

Some will tell you that wine with bubbles should be drunk from a fluted (i.e., tall, thin) glass to keep the bubbles going. But I'm prepared to go for style over practicalities and, on a Sunday, if we've got friends in, there will be fizz, and I will drink it out of a *coupe de Champagne*. This is, essentially, a boob-shaped glass, allegedly modelled on Marie Antoinette's breasts. If they had been modelled on mine, the glasses would be much bigger. In fact, the cup would runneth over. Anyway, these pretty glasses, also known as saucers, are simply beautiful to look at, especially when filled with bubbles. Prosecco, vintage Cava, Crémant or preferably Champers – whatever we've got in. As long as it's cold in the glass and delicious in the mouth, I'm a happy cook.

✳ A CHEEKY WHITE WINE

Hunger is the best sauce in the world, so goes the saying, and I have to try really hard not to consume my bodyweight in crisps/olives/nuts when preparing lunch. However, the combination of a little salted appetizer (i.e., the peanut) and a cool, crisp glass of white, all twitchy with acidity, seems to heighten the joy when you finally get to tuck in to a plate of proper food. Here I go for something more crisp and lemon-like, rather than ripe and fruity. Usual suspects include Pecorino from Italy or a Savennières (a crisp Loire Valley white made from Chenin Blanc). There is something rather refreshing about putting a bottle that's not just another Sauvignon or Chardonnay on the table.

✳ A SPIRITED PERFORMANCE

I'm not a big spirits drinker: vodka makes me feisty, gin makes me cry, whisky makes me think I'm Judi Dench. Fairly recently, someone bought me a gin martini and it made me confess how I'd once peed on a Power Plate, used in my efforts (without having to break sweat, obviously) to lose baby weight. It was the horrified look on their face that made me realize I'd overshared, crossing firmly into TMI territory.

So it is that I (relatively) rarely drink spirits and definitely not before lunch. Having said that, if we're on later lunch timings and it is nearer 6 p.m. than 1 p.m., then a proper G&T with lots of ice and a twist of lemon is sometimes, just sometimes, what's called for. Again, peanuts required.

The Husband is the youngest of four, so when it comes to eating Sunday lunch at his parents' house, there are usually two sittings, one for the children and one for the adults. You know how John Lewis is never knowingly undersold? Well, my mother-in-law is never, ever knowingly undercatered. Years of putting food on the table means that she can stretch a lunch intended for six up to eleven without so much as a sigh, and her cooking is like a culinary cuddle. There are always roast and mashed potatoes when it comes to the Sunday roast; a huge carb footprint, you might say. The Husband is incredibly greedy. When he eats, he piles his plate high, free-buffet style, then eats without stopping so that he can have seconds before it's all gone. I think this is what being the youngest of four does to a man. Even now, years after he left home, once back round that old oak table he eats in fear of there being nothing left when he finishes his plate. Scarred, I tell you.

Put simply, the bigger the flavour of your meat, the bigger the flavour of wine it can support. Once you are able to identify the difference between bigger red wines – generally you're looking at riper, often New World styles (wines from the sunny slopes of Colchagua in Chile or the Barossa Valley in Australia) or supple Old World styles (think Rioja or Cabernet-Merlot blends from Bordeaux)

– then you can start pairing wines with your Sunday roast, no sweat.

There are some things to be aware of, however; although the tannins found in red wines break down fat proteins in meat, thereby 'softening' them, sometimes tannins clash with fat. So, if you've got a fatty pork belly (not you personally) you should avoid very tannic reds such as Syrah/ Shiraz and go for a red with good acidity to cut through the fat, like a Chianti from Italy or even a red from the Loire Valley in France.

Think about the weight of the flavours from the meat – and whatever sauce is accompanying it – and try to balance it with a red that will stand up to it but not shout over it. Good examples of things to try are: beef with Shiraz/Syrah (same grape, different names, depending on where it's grown) or Cabernet Sauvignon; lamb with Tempranillo (such as Rioja); loin of pork with Gamay (try a Beaujolais Villages or Fleurie); chicken with a fuller-bodied (New World) Chardonnay or a Viognier.

Obviously there are endless possible combinations to try and this is by no means an exhaustive list. Rather, it is a starting point. So, here are some suggestions for what to put with what on a Sunday. Don't be baffled by the names – I'll explain each one as we go along.

What type of roast are you having?	What wine style to go for?	What grape variety?	Which country should I go for?	Why choose this one?
Chicken	Medium-bodied whites	Chardonnay	A wine from the Mâconnais region in Burgundy, France	Creamy, round flavours big enough to cope with the trimmings as well as the chicken
Goose	Fuller-bodied whites or medium-bodied reds	Viognier	Argentina or the Rhône region in France	Ripe, fruity, almost spicy white with a fair lick of alcohol, matches up to the earthy flavours of the meat
		Pinot Noir	New Zealand or the Burgundy region in France	Softer tannins and good acidity that cuts through the fat of the goose
Beef	Full-bodied reds	Cabernet Sauvignon	Chile, California or the Bordeaux region in France	Big tannins, big black fruits that can square up to the beefiest of roast beef
		Malbec	Argentina	Big tannins, ripe fruit, kick of spice. Argentina produces some of the world's best beef, so it's only right that they should make the perfect red wine to go with it
		Shiraz/Syrah	The Barossa region in Australia or the Rhône region in France	Big tannins, warm with lots of black fruit flavours. Loves a bit of beef, especially on the bone

What type of roast are you having?	What wine style to go for?	What grape variety?	Which country should I go for?	Why choose this one?
Lamb	Full-bodied reds	Tempranillo	Rioja region in Spain	Medium tannins, warm juicy red-fruit flavours that will work with, not against, the meat
		Sangiovese	Chianti region in Italy	Medium tannins, good acidity, which is helpful when you've got a bit of fat on the lamb
Pork	Medium-bodied reds	Gamay	Beaujolais region in France	Softer tannins, bright, often strawberry-like fruit and higher acidity, good for cutting through the fat of pork belly
Salmon	Medium-bodied reds	Pinot Noir	Germany, New Zealand or the Burgundy region in France	Lighter tannins won't overpower the flavour of the fish and good acidity will cut through oiliness
Vegetarian dishes	Medium-bodied reds	Merlot	California or Languedoc region in France	Softer tannins and plum-flesh fruit sits comfortably with most roasted vegetable-based dishes

So, the main course has been scoffed, plates piled up by the sink and the children are banging the table calling for ice cream. Now, it being Sunday and all, with school/work the next day, we don't usually pile into the dessert wines. But, if it's called for, here's what we'd have:

ICE CREAM

I've tried all sorts of wine and ice-cream combinations (I know, the things I do in the name of research – always working, that's me) and can honestly say it's mostly disastrous. Unless it's really sweet, the ice cream makes the wine taste sour. And there's no point in putting it with something too delicate as your palate is temporarily frozen. If we're going to have something grown-up with ice cream, it will be the treacle-thick, ultra-sweet Pedro Ximenez sherry (PX as it's known and sometimes labelled), simply poured over the top.

CRUMBLE

If you've got some, a dash of aged tawny port is just gorgeous with most fruit crumbles. I serve it chilled in tiny shot glasses. Don't serve it in the coupes, you'll be in all sorts of trouble. (See pages 118–120 for more details on tawny and other types of port).

CHOCOLATE BROWNIES

It's got to be a short, sharp shot of espresso over wine, unless it's vintage port, Maury or Banyuls (gorgeous, sweet fortified wines from the South of France). These were mentioned earlier when we explored the whole wine and chocolate thing (see page 103 for more suggestions, all to be tried and tasted, obviously).

* * *

So, that's Sunday lunch sorted. Every now and again, we are asked for Sunday lunch at someone's house where we're not actually related. The invitations are few and far between, admittedly, mostly because we've realized that the long five-hour, five-bottle lunches of BC (before children) are a thing of the past. And to try and replicate them with a house full of riotous children (child to adult ratio normally 2:1) is, frankly, painful. This all changes with better weather when the lunches can move outside (more on that later), but for inside, round-the-table lunches, I love them but I couldn't do them all the time.

When we do go, however, we always take wine. And if you don't know what it is you're going to be eating, I'd suggest taking something that suits both chicken or red meat, and shows that you care. I'm talking Pinot Noir, from either Burgundy or New Zealand. Even if they don't open it (which I find slightly annoying, for the record, because

I usually try and find something different and interesting which I DESPERATELY WANT TO TRY), then at least you know you've made an effort and can go home without feeling guilty about not offering to wash up.

TRUE OR FALSE? WINE IS GETTING MORE ALCOHOLIC

Yes, it has been, specifically New World wines, where the warmer climates produce wines with lots of fruit and lots of alcohol. Natural sugar levels rise as the grapes ripen, so in hotter countries, where the grapes are super ripe, the resulting wines will be higher in alcohol than in countries with cooler climates. It's also a fashionable thing: big wines with lots of flavour (i.e., alcohol, fruit and oak) stand out.

However, the tide is very definitely turning and we're now moving back from these big alcoholic styles of wine to something more subtle and less in-your-face. I want something I can still enjoy on my second glass, rather than feeling like I have to have a lie down in a darkened room between top-ups. Avoid the 14.5 per cent wines and go for something closer to 12 per cent. If you want lower still, look to wines from Germany, northern France or other cooler wine-producing areas like England. (More on this later, in chapter fourteen, by which time we'll be in the garden.)

CHAPTER

TWELVE

GROWN-UP OCCASIONS

I know that as a mother I'm supposed to know stuff. I'm supposed to know why the sky is blue. I'm supposed to know where you go when you die (and if you get there by car), and I'm supposed to know what causes a double rainbow. These are all questions recently discussed on the school run. I say discussed. It's usually more a case of me delivering cobbled-together responses whilst Eldest Boy looks at me expectantly. His questions are by far the toughest. Middle Boy's questions usually revolve around bodily functions and Youngest Girl's are mostly determined by what's happening in Peppa Pig's life. But, as grown-ups, we are supposed to know *everything*, so I deliver answers wearing my grown-up face and hope he doesn't check my facts one day and realize that, on rare occasions, I was winging it.

Here's the thing: I don't want you to have to wing it on wine any more. You now know how wine is made. You know why white wine is white, why rosé wine is pink and why red wine is red. You even know how bubbles get into wine. You know what affects how a wine tastes

– people, place and grapes – and you know that when it comes to matching food and wine, you think about the weight of the wine first. You know about the main grape varieties and you know that sometimes a blend of grapes is more interesting than a single grape variety. You know the value of the actual wine in a £5 bottle and that by spending a few quid more you get much better value for money when it comes to the quality of the wine. You know how to taste wine and you know how to scribble your thoughts down, so that you can remember what you like and don't like. But what you don't know, yet, is how to buy wine with confidence. Let's have a look at how to do that, and afterwards we'll look at buying wine for grown-up occasions.

IN A SUPERMARKET

The general approach seems to be bottom shelf for the cheap stuff, middle shelf for better everyday and top shelf for special occasions. There is something psychological in reaching down for cheap and reaching up for expensive, whilst the middle feels safe. Other than that, the chances are you're pretty much on your own. You might get lucky and find a member of staff who can tell you about the wines in the range, but more often you'll be alone, save for a few other shoppers who'll be trawling the aisle slower than they would cereals, for example.

Think about the cereal aisle. You know what to expect from a packet of Weetabix, and if you buy the supermarket own-brand version, you know it will be pretty similar (if not absolutely identical). But the average cereal aisle has a lot less for you to choose from and the brands are well known. The wine aisle will have at least five times that number of products, and the brands are few and far between. Obviously, if there is a brand on the shelf that you know and love, then you're sorted. But if you want to try something different and expand your wine horizons, it's very difficult to know where to look.

For a start the wines are often stocked on the shelf according to colour and country rather than style, leaving you no option but to go cross-country. At this point, look for a signpost. Start with a grape you like and go from there. So, if you like Pinot Grigio, go to Italy and try a different white, either a blend or a regional wine, but something that tells you it's dry and crisp (look on the back label for a description, or symbol or number describing the wine. There isn't a universal code, but many of the supermarkets use a numerical or alphabetical scale to describe the dryness/sweetness of whites and weight of reds). If you like French red, go to the region you normally buy from and pick up a bottle from another region instead.

Now, I realize I'm asking you to take a punt, and with your money, not mine, but remember that supermarket own brands are a real source of pride for them (I'm generalizing, obviously, but it is, on the whole, true). They sell brands because they have to (we want to buy them), but the real time and effort is invested in sourcing their top-tier own-brand wines. I know that because I did it.

As a wine buyer I would spend weeks scouring South America for the perfect Cabernet or blend, tasting *hundreds* of wines before finding the one that I thought was the best quality and, importantly, best value for money. Supermarket own brands are often better value than some of the big brands IMHO, and it's a good way to try something new without it being an expensive mistake if you don't like it.

Talking of making mistakes, a word on wine deals. Step into any supermarket and you will be surrounded by money-off deals. And, as mentioned before, if the offer is on a product I know and love (well, I don't actually *love* washing powder but you know what I mean) then they're going to end up in my trolley as I am saving money on a needed and known entity. However, if the offer is on something I've never tried before, and I think the original price is a little on the high side, I usually walk on by. This goes for the wine aisle too.

The definition of a good wine offer is when it's an offer on something I know, or have at least heard of, and quite fancy trying (need is stretching it). I want to feel I'm getting great value: big-name Champagne deals spring to mind. However, money off for a bottle of something I've never tried before isn't as appealing.

If you're going down this route, at least try a bottle before committing to cases of it for a party. My favourite deal is when a discount is offered across a whole range, so that I can choose which wines I want to buy. Most of the good retailers do this from time to time, usually offering around 25 per cent off, but you'll probably have to buy at least six bottles. If so, go for a few firm favourites but take a punt and try something new for at least a few bottles. Just beware that sometimes the deal really is too good to be true – that practically half-price Pinot Grigio was pushing it at £12 in the first place.

WINE SHOPS

Generally, people who work in wine shops love wine. Most of them love drinking it and most of them love talking about it. If you've taken the trouble to go to a wine shop and aren't just buying wine in the supermarket along with the rest of your groceries, then I'm assuming you are in slightly less of a hurry to get in and out. Unless you've got children in tow: children and bottles at low shelf height are a dangerous combination, only slightly less hazardous than being in the John Lewis crockery department with a three-year-old.

If you have got time then ask questions. Tell them what you usually drink and ask if they can recommend something similar that you haven't tried before. Experiment, go crazy, be brave. Remember that the range before you will have been put together by someone who's unusually nuts about wine; they will probably have tried every single wine and know the story behind each one.

That's the best bit when choosing a new wine: finding out about who made it, why they made it and what they say about it. Too often, we don't get to find out the story behind a wine, and yet it's almost always more memorable when we know about the people who made the stuff. A good wine shop will have people who know this and they will love seeing you leave with something you've never tried before only to come back for more.

Avoid the bottles with dust on, though: they've obviously been sitting there a while. Having said that, the bottles with dust on in supermarkets are often the hidden gems on the top shelf with a fairly hefty price tag. When they are sold through as a bin-end (a name given to the last few remaining bottles of wine from a particular collection, which are usually sold at a big discount), the dust-covered bottle can come good.

ONLINE

This is a great way to buy wine – from the sofa (brilliant!). It also means you can wander off on a fact-finding thread about a particular wine without having to actually get up. Online wine shops are popping up all over the place and the good ones tell you about the people behind the wine, giving them a real sense of place. Most of the supermarkets have their own wine websites, with brief but to-the-point tasting notes and all sorts of other stuff, such as food and wine matching, recommendations from newspaper wine experts and buying guides. But there is also a raft of online-specific wine retailers that is worth exploring.

One of the most useful tools is reading what other customers have said about a wine. Obviously, one person's favourite is another's most revolting, but at least it's a signpost of sorts. Obviously, standards vary enormously, but the good ones are really good.

IN A RESTAURANT

Due to the line of work I am in, I don't often have to fight over the wine list with my restaurant companion, be it the Husband ('You don't have to read the *whole* thing'), mother ('Anything but Chardonnay, unless it's Chablis') or friend ('Does that come in a big glass?') but if you aren't usually the one to choose, make sure you become the one who grabs the wine list, and don't feel rushed. Experience is all and knowledge is power. I am aware that I'm sounding like a fortune cookie.

Assuming you know what you're eating, you can choose the colour of the wine you're going to have – or at least start with – and work your way down. House wines are going to be good but probably not memorable, a safe bet if you like. But we're getting out of that comfort zone, remember? So, don't always go for the house wine. If you're feeling even slightly flush (you are in a restaurant, after all), then try something new. Not the most expensive stuff – that's there for the dudes trying to impress dates/work colleagues – no, what you need to do is cherry pick, and having a bit of wine knowledge helps you do just that. There is almost always a bargain to be had on a wine list, you just need to know how to find it.

Again, ask questions if the wine guy/lady sounds like they know their stuff. If they are really trying to sell you a particular bottle, ask to try a bit first. If not, buy it by the glass and try out a few different wines around the table. If you're having a wine that's sold by the glass it's worth asking how long the bottle has been open – nicely, of course, but sometimes they can be left open for more than a few days. You shouldn't be afraid to ask; you are paying for it, after all. If in doubt, go for more recent vintages rather than older vintages as younger wine is generally less risky.

SPECIAL-OCCASION STUFF

I like to think we learn from experience. In fact, I was once asked what experience has shaped me the most and why. I've got two.

Firstly, meeting my husband-to-be at four years old and being together from the age of fifteen; I think that growing up with the person I went on to marry has shaped who I am. Two decades of marriage and three children later, I still feel like a teenager. Sometimes, when our children wander into our bedroom in the morning, all bed hair and sleepy-eyed, it takes me a second to register that I am in fact a grown-up and that we've got children, a house, a dog and a lawn that needs mowing.

Secondly, my little brother died in 2002. It was very sudden and shocking and he was only twenty-six years old. It has taken a while, but honestly, I can now say he has saved me from sweating the small stuff for the rest of my life. He's also made us, as a family, really good at celebrating life at any given opportunity, just as he did. Whether it's birthdays, anniversaries, new babies, new jobs, a new house, whatever; a bottle of wine bought with that person in mind and a big hug when it is given is one of the most perfect, life-affirming presents I can think of. Here's what to buy, when:

✳ BIRTHDAYS

Obviously it helps if you know what the person you are buying for likes, but if you don't, think of it as an opportunity to go crazy and get them something that says, 'I think you are ace.' Here are just a few options for 'I think you are ace' wines:

Rhône

If the recipient loves big reds, here's where to go. A red from the northern Rhône Valley, such as Côte Rôtie, made predominantly from the Syrah grape, will set you back about £20. Vintage-wise, 2007 is the year to go for.

Burgundy

Something made from the Pinot Noir grape (as red Burgundy is) says, 'You're fab.' It also says, 'I know it's expensive, but you, my friend, are worth it.' The same goes for a white, which will be made from the Chardonnay grape. You're looking at spending at least £15–20. Remember, Burgundy is a bit of a minefield, with thousands of different producers and over one hundred different appellations (regions within a region), so buy with care.

Bordeaux

This is the big one, the so-called king of wine regions (self-appointed, obviously), associated with grand chateaux and beautifully manicured vineyards, as well as some of the most expensive wines in the world. But, with a bit of skill and luck on your side, you can find some wonderful red wines here that the recipient will love, as well as making you look like an impressive wine buff. Go for right bank (meaning wines from St Emilion or Pomerol if possible) with 2008 or 2006 on the label.

✳ LANDMARK BIRTHDAYS (ONES ENDING IN AN '0')

Time to go for something with a vintage writ large on the label (the year telling you which year the grapes were harvested). And nothing says you are grown up and getting on a bit like a bottle of port. So, vintage port from a reputable producer, and you're looking at spending around £30 (landmark, remember).

✳ ANNIVERSARIES

This one is all about the love, and few things are more *amore* than pink Champagne. If it's a significant anniversary, I go vintage (see page 153 for more information about vintage Champagne) and, although expensive, at least I know I'm getting half of it. Pair it with fish and chips for pure romantic decadence.

✳ NEW GODCHILD/BABY

You could buy them a bottle of something that will age, so they can drink it when they're eighteen or twenty-one, although I know a bottle of vintage port would have been (in fact, was) completely wasted on me at that age. I did buy a bottle of Sauternes (the sweet noble-rotted white from Bordeaux that we've talked about) for a goddaughter recently, not least so I could write 'a sweetie for a sweetie' in the card. But seriously, I think it's better to buy a bottle of fizz for the parents and turn up on the doorstep with that in one hand and a home-made lasagne in the other.

✳ MOTHER'S/FATHER'S DAY

I'm at the stage where my mother's day present is usually a collection of drawings of skateboarders, dinosaurs or rainbows, together with a cup of tea brought to me in bed. I'm happy with that, but for my own mother, it's always a bottle of something with bubbles, because I know that's what she loves and because I get to drink it with her. She likes a fuller, richer style of Champagne rather than an elegant, crisp one, so I usually go for a Pinot Noir/ Chardonnay blend with a bit of age. (For tips on what to get in – or ask to be got in – for Mother's Day lunch, see chapters six and eleven.)

For my father, it's always a bottle of red to go with lunch, and seeing as he's an all-weather barbecue man (he even has a little porch just outside the back door so he can keep dry while cooking), it's usually a fairly punchy red, something from the Rhône or Australia with Syrah/Shiraz as the main grape.

RING THE CHANGES

Have a look at the list overleaf to get you in the mood for trying something different, with confidence:

✳ WHITE WINES

If you like . . .	Then try . . .	Why?
Fruity Chardonnay	Marsanne or Roussane from the South of France	Same warm peachy fruit, but the grape varieties are less well known. I promise you they can be utterly delicious
Not-too-fruity Chardonnay	Cortese from Italy	Gavi, for example, is just one Italian dry white that does fresh fruit, but not in an in-your-face way
Sauvignon Blanc	Rueda from Spain	Light, lemony and refreshingly different. Rueda is the region, so look for this on the label. Verdejo is the grape
Pinot Grigio	Another crisp dry white from Italy (Greco, Vermentino, Falanghina, Cortese, Fiano, I could go on)	Because Pinot Grigio is fine, but there are so many other delicious Italian whites to try . . . and so little time
Riesling	Pinot Gris from New Zealand	If you like Riesling, then you might not want to change at all. But if you do, try a Pinot Gris (same grape as Pinot Grigio but more French in style). Classically beautiful

✳ RED WINES

If you like . . .	Then try . . .	Why?
Cabernet Sauvignon	Malbec from Argentina	Big, bold and just a little warmer in style. Will make you want to dance, possibly even tango
Merlot	Grenache (probably blended with Syrah and Mourvèdre) from the South of France	Same soft red fruits with added sunshine and oomph. Here, the sum is very definitely greater than the parts
Shiraz	Syrah from the northern Rhône	Same grape, but French ones from the Rhône Valley tend to have a sort of 'coolness' to them, both in terms of climate versus Australia, and in the style of the wine. Not so shouty, but lots to shout about, if you see what I mean
Tempranillo	Tempranillo from Ribero del Duero	If you like Rioja, try the reds from here. You're still in Spain, just trying something different

CHAPTER

THIRTEEN

THE SCHOOL FÊTE
(ACCOMPLI)

The summer term is a demanding one, not least because with the evenings being lighter the children take *for ever* to go to sleep at night (should have kept those blackout blinds). That, and the endless call for cake donations for cricket teas, charity sales and, of course, the school fête. Now, I do love a bake-off under normal circumstances, but sometimes, when the request comes home for cake at short notice, I resort to the fake bake. This involves offering my mother/mother-in-law/stepmother their wine of choice (and I know all their weak spots) in return for a plate of fairy cakes. For the school fête, however, it's usually all mine and Betty Crocker's own work (she makes possibly the best ready-to-scoff chocolate fudge icing ever created), together with a large dose of sprinkles.

One of my favourite stalls at the school fête is the second-hand-toy stall; it's such a fantastic opportunity to get rid of big plastic musical keyboards. You know, the ones the children hardly ever play with, but which take up loads of space in the kitchen/playroom. One year, I gave away a big plastic musical keyboard, only for us to be given another one as a hand-me-down. I duly gave that one away at the next fête. A card-carrying organ donor, that's me.

Other stalwart stalls at the fête include the raffle, the lucky dip, the home-made cake stall and, of course, guess the number of sweets in the jar. Let's look at these more closely from a wine perspective.

THE RAFFLE

This is an excellent opportunity to donate unwanted wine as a prize. You may well win it back again, but at least you tried. I'm talking about the random bottle of wine you were given years ago, you can't remember who by, and it stayed in the rack because every time you've pulled it out since, you've taken a look at the label and thought, 'Nah, not that desperate.' It's an unknown quantity, possibly German, so you're not sure if it's sweet or dry. It might be French, but it's so 'country' looking you suspect it might strip the roof of your mouth of any feeling. It might even be the one you bought back from holiday years ago. Actually, you bought two bottles back, but the first was such a disappointment, nothing like as delicious as when you sipped it in the shade overlooking the sea, that the other bottle has remained unopened (more on this in a moment).

If you've got this bottle in your rack, here's what you should do. Wrap it in bright tissue paper, dress it up with ribbon, bows, anything to make it look good, and put a neck tag on it with the words 'Drink Me' beautifully printed, à la *Alice in Wonderland*. Just make sure the donation is anonymous and be prepared to win it back. In which case, stick it back in the rack until next year and remember to change the wrapping to avoid your cover being blown. Think of it as the wine equivalent of the plastic musical keyboard.

THE LUCKY DIP

This used to be my absolute favourite as a child, because it was one of the cheapest per go and, best of all, you always won. In fact, I couldn't understand why people would want to waste their money on trying to hook a duck, or win on a coconut shy when, with a lucky dip, you win every time. I do like certainty (did I mention I'm Virgo?).

When it comes to wine, there are occasions when I'm prepared to take a risk and delve into the wine lucky dip, because if I don't, I might be missing out on the most delicious wine and I'd never know it. I realize that I'm pretty well equipped to work my way around the wine maze that is the supermarket shelf, the wine list or the specialist wine shop equivalent of Aladdin's cave, but because there's so much choice when it comes to wine – a ridiculous amount really – even I get lost on occasion. I really do have to find out what I can from the labels (often not that easy, as we've seen) and then just go with my gut feel. It's a bit of a lucky dip, except that sometimes it might turn out to be unlucky, in which case, I make a (mental/posh-notebook) note and don't make that mistake again.

With the school fête lucky dip, you're really shopping blind, but with wine there *are* pointers – country, region, grape – to help you. You might not win every time, but at least you're trying something different and you might unearth a gem. I'll take wine over a lollipop any time.

THE CAKE STALL

I love this stall. In the old days, as a child, I remember seeing a table covered in Victoria sponges, but as our nation's obsession with baking has taken hold – coupled with the naturally competitive nature of the school fête cake stall – the table is now as likely to be covered with towers of cupcakes, enormous strawberry-stacked, multi-layered sponges and enough chocolate brownies to sink a ship. Consequently, my Betty Crocker-covered chocolate mash-up is usually bought by someone I'm related to, possibly out of pity. There's nothing worse than your cake being the last one left on the table, reduced for quick sale.

Now, of course, cakes must be labelled with all the ingredients. Nuts aside, I would have thought butter, flour, eggs and sugar was enough, but apparently not. The same is happening for wine. As it stands, wine doesn't require a list of ingredients on the back label, apart from 'contains sulphites'. What this means is a small amount of sulphur-based chemicals are added to the wine in order to stop it oxidizing (going brown). Sulphites are used in all sorts of food groups as a preserving agent, including dried fruits, processed meats, chips, ketchup and lots of fruit squashes and cordials. All wines contain at least a small amount of sulphites as they're a natural result of the fermentation process. What isn't on the label is the other stuff, apart from grapes, which is used to make wine. That might include yeast, tartaric acid (the same stuff usually found in baking soda) and tannin additions (usually in powder form).

Wine is not yet required to include these other additions on the back labels when sold in the UK, but they might yet go the way of school-fête cakes and require more descriptive labelling eventually. Until then, if you want to buy a wine and know that the ingredients are nothing but grapes, then you need to give natural wines a try.

WHAT ARE 'NATURAL' WINES?

Natural wines are those made with as little intervention as possible, either in the vineyard or in the winery. The movement dates back to the 1970s, particularly to the Loire and Beaujolais regions of France, but it's grown to embrace winemakers all over the place who want to do things as naturally as possible.

The wines are usually made from organically or even bio-dynamically grown grapes (sort of superorganic, if you like, a more holistic approach), meaning, ideally, no chemicals or additives. However, some are more 'natural' than others, depending on the winemaker. Some may choose to add a bit of sulphur dioxide when they bottle the wine to keep it fresh, for example. The point is, the wine is usually made in small quantities, and is often pretty unique in taste.

Some natural wines I've tried are a bit too feral for me, but generally the really good ones are exactly that: really good wines with wonderful flavours. The fact that they are natural is even better. The problem is finding them – you'll need to venture beyond most supermarket shelves for these wines – but such is the interest in the natural wine movement that more and more independent, specialist and online wine shops are getting behind them.

You're looking at spending at least a tenner on a bottle and, whatever you do, don't leave these ones in the rack for too long. In my experience they're usually better drunk young than left to age for too long. Definitely worth a go, though it's back to the wine lucky-dip principle: some prizes are better than others.

GUESS HOW MANY SWEETS IN THE JAR?

It must be said that I've never won this – they don't even make it multiple choice! – so to make it easier, here's a quick 'guess how many . . .' for you, about wine. Multiple choice, obvs.

Q: Guess how many bubbles there are in a bottle of Champagne?
   a) 50 million
   b) 150 million
   c) 250 million
   d) None

A: None, until you open the bottle (ha!). Then there's about 50 million in there, apparently.

GEARING UP FOR THE HOLIDAYS

Let's go back to holiday wines for a moment. We've all had a holiday romance, where we've sworn absolute undying love when we're out there. But once back on home ground, without the sun, sea (or even ski) views, the object of our affection seems to fade as quickly as our tans. I had my own particular summer romance with a Turkish rosé. I'm yet to find it here (although some Turkish wines are definitely improving in quality, and more are finding their way onto wine shop shelves and wine lists). Then there was a fling with Retsina (I can't be the only one). Even an undiscovered sherry gem turned out to taste better in the sunshine than back here at home. Clearly, I was blinded by price.

For sure, there are some holiday wine romances that will stay the course, but most turn out to be a not-very-fine wine romance. So, how do you avoid having your heart broken? And how do you find lasting love?

If you've been into a French hypermarket, or *'ee-permar-shay* as they say, you'll know that it makes the wall of wine in our supermarkets look small by comparison. They really do stack 'em up and pack 'em in, with barrels and plastic grapes at every turn. The choice is enormous and, of course, mostly French. The problem is, with so much to choose from it's easier to fall prey to wine that is, to be honest, just a little bit *merde*. Don't buy in quantity unless you have tried it, even if that means buying a bottle one day and returning to stock up the next. So far, when I've suggested you try a Gigondas for example (a red wine from the Rhône Valley), I know that in any given supermarket in the UK you will only have a couple to choose from, and in most cases the wines will have been through a pretty rigorous tasting process to make it onto the shelves in the first place, thanks to the generally demanding wine buyers we've got here.

In France, you will have more choice but that also means that, with wines from lots of different producers, the quality will vary more. You've just got to be prepared to take a risk, so it really is worth trying a bottle before buying a case.

For good, inexpensive holiday wines, I suggest buying local. If you find yourself in a pretty town in Europe (or on the campsite just outside that pretty town), go native and see what you find. As if by magic, wines from a particular area often perfectly match the foods from the same area. For example, in the Loire Valley is a little village called Chavignol, where they make Crottin de Chavignol, a soft goat's cheese that loves wine with acidity. Coincidentally, the nearest wine region is Sancerre, famous for producing – guess what? – dry whites from the Sauvignon Blanc grape with crisp acidity.

Think of Italy with all those mind-bendingly good tomato-based pasta dishes. What they need is a red with acidity (remember, tomatoes are high in acidity). And as it happens, Sangiovese, the main ingredient for wines from Chianti, is known for producing wines with high acidity (also good for cutting through creamy carbonara-type dishes). In my experience, holiday wine tends not to travel well and is best enjoyed in situ. And if it is really horrible, wrap it up and bring it back for the school raffle. Fête accompli.

Time to go into the garden.

TRUE OR FALSE? 'LEGS' ON A GLASS ARE A SIGN OF QUALITY

I have seen the legs in a glass of wine reduce a man to tears of joy, in a 'Will you look at the legs on that?' kind of way. He wasn't talking about the same legs bearded wonders ZZ Top sang about, but the effect is not dissimilar, clearly. What he was talking about is the candlestick drip-like effect left as the wine drips down the inside of the glass after it's been given a really good swirl. *Those* legs. So what do legs on a glass of wine mean? Well, mostly they tell you the wine has got lots of alcohol and sugar in it; port and sweet wines such as Sauternes have really noticeable legs. Most wines, however, don't. Some might leave a fleeting trace on the glass, but again these will be the ones with more sugar and/or alcohol in them. It's not necessarily a guide to quality, more a guide to the type of wine you're about to drink. Another myth debunked. You're welcome.

CHAPTER

FOURTEEN

IN THE (DAY OR NIGHT) GARDEN

SUMMER WHAT I LOVE

Sun on skin. A sea breeze. Picnics on the beach. Children in towelling robes. Rock pooling. Crabbing. Scones and clotted cream. Hotdogs for tea. Clinky drinks with ice. Very chilled white wine. A really tart salad dressing. Barbecued meat. Red wine in small tumblers. Tealights. Talking into the night.

SUMMER WHAT I DON'T LOVE

Sand in the sandwiches. Wasps. Warm wine.

* * *

When school's out and the holidays stretch before us, I am filled with excitement. OK, I am also filled with a slight dread at how I'm going to pull off part-time work with a house full of children, but we manage it in a chaotic kind of way. When I think back to my own childhood, much of my summer was spent crabbing on the pontoon on the nearby river. Together with my brother and sister, we would spend hours pulling up tiny crabs lured onto the line with old bacon, collecting them in a bucket, only to pour them all back into the sea when our stash reached admirable levels. Then we'd start all over again. There was no point to catching the crabs – they were too small to eat – it was just fun.

As a result, I am all for my children doing as many pointless pursuits as they wish; the more the better. We don't get to do them much, if at all, as adults so I want them to make the most of it now. Jumping through the sprinkler in the garden is a particular favourite, closely followed by setting traps for robbers. Tiger Mom would be horrified.

Now, cast your mind back to what I told you about what makes a wine a *good* wine. I realize this was some time ago and that some of us have trouble remembering why we went into a particular room in the house, let alone recalling something I told you about wine at the start of the book, back when your lab coat was wine-spotless and your pencil was still sharp. We're talking balance. That is, how the different parts – alcohol, sweetness, acidity and tannins – sit together in the wine. When the components come together and strike a natural balance, good things can happen. It they don't – the fruit is shouted down by the oaky character, say, or the alcohol leaves a hot sensation in the mouth (sorry, I seem to have gone a bit *Fifty Shades*) – then the wine just doesn't work as well.

Essentially, it's all about balance. And so it is with my life. A question of balance, that is. And one of the things that really helped me achieve greater balance was letting go of the magazine cover image of entertaining in the garden.

In my dreams, our garden is framed by wild flowers. In reality, it's dotted with footballs and abandoned bicycles. Dream garden has cornflowers in recycled, label-less tin cans with stripy Provence-style table linen, paper lanterns in the trees and a sheepskin-floored yurt to one side. Real garden has a weather-beaten table and a few matching chairs left, patches of bare grass due to heavy ball-game activity and a broken rope ladder. I did manage to plant a couple of Ikea pots with lavender, but that's about as Sarah Raven as it gets.

Nevertheless, eating outside as a family is one of my favourite things, and as long as you get the right combination of people, food and wine, no one even notices the lack of bunting. We've had the same small charcoal barbecue for years, the Husband refusing to resort to gas (that's cheating, surely. Man must control fire. Or at least use up half a bottle of lighter fluid). And once we've used the barbecue for the first time each summer, so most of our meals are cooked on it until September comes and the novelty has worn off.

Proper charcoaled, flame-grilled food needs wine with lots of flavour. But summer salads and lighter dishes need wines that are lighter in character. Match like with like, remember. We'll come back to food matching in a moment, but first, let's trip the light wine fantastic.

LIGHTER WINE STYLES

When the weather is hot, hot, hot (ever the optimist), chunky reds don't cut it, at least not until there's a plate of barbecued meat on the table. Pre-meat, I usually want something white or pink, possibly with bubbles, and with slightly lower alcohol levels. I'm not talking about the lower-alcohol wines we covered earlier, but the ones made from grapes that produce wines of around 12 per cent or lower naturally.

✳ MUSCADET

Made from the Melon de Bourgogne grape in the Loire Valley, France, these wines are often underrated and forgotten about. The good ones are light, fresh, lemony and really refreshing, and they won't be more than 12 per cent alcohol.

✳ VINHO VERDE

Sadly, the Portuguese white wines carrying this name are a bit hard to find nowadays, but they're really worth seeking out. Vinho Verde means 'green wine', but this doesn't refer to the colour, rather to the fact that the wine is best quaffed young, while it's still loaded with lemon fruit and a gentle natural spritz. Alcohol levels vary but are usually around 9 per cent. Properly heavenly with grilled sardines.

✳ MOSCATO

This is a catch-all name for slightly sweet, lightly fizzy, pink or white wine made from the muscat grape. Some are frothy, fun and fit-for-purpose but they are often just as forgettable. If you want to try something really delicious, then Moscato d'Asti with the DOCG stamp (telling you it's from a recognized top-quality region in Italy) is the one to go for.

This is one to drink before food, or it can be saved until the summer pudding hits the table. Honestly, the best way to describe it is grapey. Freshly crushed grapes, in fact. And the alcohol is around 5.5 per cent, so nice and light.

✳ RIESLING

There are some gorgeous dry and off-dry German Rieslings that come in at about 8 per cent, neatly falling into my naturally lighter wine category. Find one from the Mosel region and you'll probably find a wine with finely balanced lime fruit and sharp acidity, sometimes set off with a bit of sweetness. They work a treat with Asian food. If you're confused by the label and want a dry or off-dry Riesling (and German wine labels are amongst the most confusing) then look out for the words 'trocken' (meaning dry) or 'kabinett' for the sort of wine I'm talking about here.

✳ ENGLISH WINE

As mentioned earlier, English wine is undergoing something of a revolution and learning to love itself. Over the last few years, healthy grapes have resulted in better wines, and because of our (cough) cool climate, the natural sugars aren't huge, so the resulting alcohol levels are modest. Some of the more widely available English dry white wines come in at around 11–12 per cent, including rosé wine.

✳ REDS

Most red wines are between 12 and 14 per cent, and as our global taste for softer, riper styles of wine has grown, so too have the number of wines with alcohol levels nearer 14 than 12 per cent. If you want to seek out reds with alcohol levels nearer 12 per cent, think cool, as in climate. Look to the Loire Valley in northern France, where some of the red wines (made from the Cabernet Franc grape) are naturally lower in alcohol. And closer to home, Pinot Noir from vineyards in England and Wales are definitely worth a go, with alcohol levels usually around 12 per cent.

JUST CHILLING

On a really hot day, a warm red wine just isn't going to cut it. As mentioned before (see page 48), the French have a long tradition of serving some of their lighter red wines, particularly those from Beaujolais, slightly chilled. Not only does it make the flavours pop, it makes the wine all the more refreshing on a hot day. Stick them in the fridge or the ice bucket for half an hour before drinking. Cool, eh? Just as dim lighting masks imperfections, so does chilling a red wine.

GREAT BARBECUE-FRIENDLY WINES

So, as the sun glints off the discarded bikes and I ask the children not to use my two lavender-filled plant pots as goalposts, my thoughts invariably turn to what wines to serve with the array of barbecued meats that will shortly be put before us. There will be chicken drumsticks, sausages, or – if we're feeding more than just us – a butterflied, sacrificial leg of lamb. There'll also be couscous salad, new potato salad, tomato salad and a green salad. This all calls for wine, but different dishes call for different wines. Obviously the barbecued food will have that chargrilled taste to it, so the wines need to be able to cope with that. But it's as much about the marinades as it is about the cooking, as this will affect the end flavour, particularly if it's a spicy or mustard-based marinade. Here's a quick guide to what wine works well with which barbecue foods:

What food?	What wine?	Why?
Chargrilled vegetables	Provence or Spanish rosé	Has enough weight to cope with the charcoal flavours and enough acidity to keep the tastes fresh
Salmon kebabs	Sauvignon Blanc if herby, dry Riesling if chilli-flecked, young Pinot Noir if really spicy	You need a wine with acidity and freshness here, something that won't dominate the fish
Burgers	Californian or French Syrah, South African Pinotage, Californian Zinfandel or Malbec	Big flavours – especially if you top the burger with cheese and/or bacon – need a wine with guts. These ones are willing to have a go
Sausages	Southern French red or Spanish Tempranillo	You need something with fruit but not too much tannin as it will clash with the fat in the sausages
Spicy chicken drumsticks	Chardonnay with a bit of oak or a Viognier	Yes, you can go for whites with barbecued meats, but they need lots of flavour if they're going to be heard over the flavours of the food
Lamb	Spanish red or southern Italian red	We need soft, juicy, warm reds for the lamb. These ones are ideal
Pork chops	Gamay (including Beaujolais Villages) or Grenache	Pork is lighter in flavour (unless you've covered it in a mustard marinade), so the bright flavours of Gamay or Grenache are a great fit
Steaks	Argentinian Malbec or Chilean Carménère	Malbec is an obvious bedfellow because of its weight, but Carménère can do the job too

So that's you all set for a summer of (wine) lovin'. Here's to warm days. But not warm wine.

Isn't that a pip?

THE LAST DROP

We've talked about a lot of different styles of wine. These are just ideas, all tried and tested, and aimed to give you a steer if you want some wine inspiration. To find the wines we've covered, simply go to the wine website of the place you shop and type in the grape variety. See what comes up and find out a bit about the wine before you go and buy it. Of course, if you're buying from your local wine shop you can ask for help finding them and for specific recommendations. As we've already established, the majority of people who work in wine shops are dying to talk about wine, you just need to ask. And don't get the equivalent of hairdresser paralysis and freeze when asked what you'd like and how much you want to spend. Instead, have a maximum price in mind before you start, tell them what sort of thing you're looking for (cue to take out your posh notebook) and off you go.

There is so much more I could tell you, but what you've got here is the need-to-know stuff. Your wine satnav is now sufficiently preloaded and you are ready for the journey, so I'll leave you to it. Here's what I'm really hoping we've achieved:

1. You are inspired to try new and different wines, not just stick to what you know.
2. You have a better idea of what to look for when

you are standing at the foot of the wall of wine.

3. You will confidently reach for the wine list next time you are eating out and won't just go for the second one down.

4. You will keep glasses of forgettable wine consumed to an absolute minimum.

And don't forget, (almost) every week I add at least a couple of wines that I've tried and tasted to my website, as well as sharing details about life as a knackered mother (I promise it's funnier than it sounds). Please come and join the club (www.knackeredmotherswineclub.com); there's loads of other stuff on there too, including links to videos about how to taste wine and how to avoid hangovers among other things. Yes, it might stop you from doing something properly productive and useful, but I do like to think I'm providing an essential service, namely stopping you from drinking bad wine.

Because, as we know, life is too short to drink bad wine.

THE KNACKERED MOTHER'S MUST-HAVE WINE LIST

FURTHER READING

If you're interested in learning more about wine, then I highly recommend the following books:

* **The Oxford Companion to Wine** – edited by Jancis Robinson. Once called the greatest wine book of all time. I agree. It's a huge book, but one I go back to, always. If it's too heavy-duty, go for her *Wine Course* book instead

* **The Concise World Atlas of Wine** – Hugh Johnson and Jancis Robinson. I do love a map and this book's full of them. It shows you places and even specific vineyards in enormous detail

WINE COURSES

If you want to go one step further and actually do a wine course, then you need to get in touch with the Wines & Spirit Education Trust (WSET). They run courses all around the country and you can study at all levels, from a basic certificate up to diploma level. See **www.wsetglobal.com** for full information on courses.

ACKNOWLEDGEMENTS

Firstly, I would like to thank my husband, Ross, for taking the children off every Saturday morning, without fuss, for the six months that it took me to write this first time round. I promise I did not lie on the sofa with a book the minute you were gone. OK, once, but only for about an hour.

I'd like to thank the brilliant team at Bluebird – Hockley, Carole and Jodie. And to my wonderful agent Heather Holden-Brown for her unwavering love and support.

Thank you, too, to everyone who reads my blog. I started writing it back in 2009 and because of you, it's grown into something that allows me to write and talk about wine for a living. I really appreciate all your comments and love being able to help with your wine-related questions.

Finally, enormous thanks to my family for letting me think I'm really interesting when I talk about wine. I love you all.

INDEX